UNSURVIVABLE IGNORANCE

The Raw Truth About
The Black Girl Curse, Globalism &
Why We Are All Called Monkeys

CONTAINS ADULT LANGUAGE

ERIC CULPEPPER

In The Wind Productions

Publisher: In The Wind Productions

ISBN: 978-1-9851780-1-4
ISBN: 1-9851780-1-X

CONTENTS

ABOUT THE COVER

THE IMAGE ON THE cover of this book is a Monkey King riding high atop an ancient Indian battle elephant and it is used here to symbolize the fact that the individuals who are in fact invisibly standing on top of the world are totally inconceivably highly militant Indians and Pakistanis who have managed to wage a very long, drawn out war for global conquest that has in fact spanned multiple entire human civilizations, encompassed the entire world and seen this omni-dimensional, totally inconceivably highly predatory culture infiltrate and gain complete control of the entire religious, technical and hyper-industrialized world without anyone ever even remotely suspecting that it is in fact the ancient Indians who have long traveled to and fro in the world and up and down in it and managed to covertly influence every government in the recorded history of the world and subsequently completely reshape the modern world in India's image.

DEDICATION

THIS BOOK IS FIRSTLY dedicated to the countless individuals from all walks of life who are making tremendous efforts to try to make positive change within the world in general.

This book is secondly dedicated to a concerned Thai Mother, whom I encountered many years ago during one of my innumerable flights to Japan where I had a residence for nearly two decades, whom, like many other Asians that I encountered during my residency in Asia, had several questions about why the Vietnam War was deemed necessary... So I covered the real reasons that The Vietnam War was deemed a necessity by those who in fact run The U.S. Government and many of other Secret Organizations and Satellite Nations from the shadows.

This book is also dedicated to my First Pimpnological Master, Master Henry Roberts of West Memphis, Arkansas., who chose me as his disciple, endowed me with extremely great general and pimpnological direction and was kind enough to have sprinkled me with that ol' black magic at the very tender age of eleven.

And this book is ultimately dedicated to, and has been composed primarily for the benefit of, truly sensible young people from all walks of life who have a sincere interest in clearly understanding their collective past, understanding how their collective past has the power to directly affect their present and whom likewise have a sincere interest in clearly understanding and properly preparing themselves for what we can presently foresee of the future.

FOREWORD

AS A GRAND INQUISITOR level disciple of an extremely ancient lineage of masters who are culturally obsessed with the accomplishment of Complete Control, the capturing of souls and how to make people completely turn their back on everything that they have ever known and valued in life I have a very special tactical interest in gaining as great a level of comprehension of the morbid intricacies of predicting the behavior of animate entities as is humanly possible and to that end I have spent more than thirty years engaged in very painstakingly in-depth and meticulous research into the most daunting aspects of human behavior spanning from what ultimately makes people hate, exploit and behave inhumanely to others, even to their own self-detriment, to the reasons why modern Americans have become so prone to family dysfunction and why black people have been totally unable to succeed in industrialized civilization and I have cracked them wide open.

However, there is another constant human behavioral anomaly that I have spent decades looking into, and that is the penchant of industrialized nations to attack and attempt to control their neighbors, even halfway around the globe far beyond the reach of their command, control and supply lines and regardless of how many young lives or how much money, national prestige or awe-inspiring hypocrisy have to be fed into the international war machine.

For as long as there has been recorded history, secret organizations have stood behind those in power and used them as puppets to mindlessly do the will of their unseen masters whom have come to be referred to as the mythological they and them who in fact run societies and it has long been wondered, exactly who are these people, what is the true source of their power and influence and why is it so vital that they function in total secrecy, however, this book goes exponentially further than merely searching for answers to long unanswered vital questions in that it clearly identifies the single culture that is in fact behind the people who are behind the military-industrial complex and the secret organizations that have long run governments and determined the fate of human civilization.

In this in depth work about the very real Phantom Menace that has plagued humanity for innumerable millennia, it is my sole aim to clearly identify the extremely ancient and inconceivably highly refined militant culture that is solely responsible for the relentless demoralization, enslavement, robbery and repetitive debilitation of and hatred against Blacks and Asians as well as all of the pain, misery, death and distress that mankind has ever known in our entire recorded history and precisely why we have been made to suffer it.

Since time immemorial there has existed an exceedingly ancient but not very well known culture called the Brahmans, which means, the ultimate reality underlying all phenomena. On the surface Brahmanism simply appears to be just another exotic Eastern religion, however, if inspected more closely one will find that it is in fact a culture that is omni-dimensional to the point that it can only be properly described as being exponentially multifaceted.

As a dimension of the ancient Hindu Religion, which is also exponentially multifaceted, Brahmanism is an elitist culture that specializes in infiltration and over countless millennia it has found its way over, under, around and through everything and is manned by some of the world's most highly calculating individuals. In Hindu religious works of art there are many militant Gods that possess multiple arms and devour their enemies, which can also very effectively be accomplished via covert activity in which numerous people stand behind each other in the dark, these are very real pictographic images of how this culture has unsuspectingly functioned for thousands of years without anyone having any real awareness of it which is a grand testament to its innumerable millennia of experience.

During the latter part of the 20th Century, a little more than a decade after the civil rights movement, there suddenly emerged a radical culture of elder and child abuse and abandonment, female gangs, gangster rap, mass-fratricide, mass-incarceration, mass-dishonorable discharge from the military and a culture of epidemic sodomy, lesbianism, substance abuse and suicidal depression, especially among black women, and this book is designed to get to the real core source of this culture that had never existed within Black America on a national scale.

THE GREAT DEBATE

I AM OFTEN COMPLETELY amazed at the miniscule length of human recollection, I'm amazed at how almost no one can clearly remember what happened even thirty five years ago in their own personal life experience. And as a direct result of the total incapability of people to recall anything I have felt the need to compose this vitally important historical work.

Though the nineteen Seventies are less than forty years behind us there is already extremely heated debate, especially among young black women, over what actually occurred during the Seventies to cause such a tremendous amount of division between black men and women that even the election of a Black President and First Lady in the person of First Family Barack and Michelle Obama has not been enough to bring black men and women back together.

Given the fact that much of the industrialized world is only given what is the functional equivalent of a cheap plastic token education that is solely for the benefit of capitalist exploiters, people absolutely do not realize that there are in fact consequences for both our individual and collective actions, consequences that have the very real power to affect us and our children for generations.

It was absolutely no secret in the Seventies that there was a hideous, irreverent, completely irrational, tremendously pride based gender separatist movement among government assistance backed urban black women who have in fact spent more than fifty years cursing, abusing, assaulting and exploiting everyone around them and claiming that they are strong, totally independent black women who are never going to need a man of any kind for anything under any circumstances no matter what eventuality presents itself while the divorce and illegitimate child birth rates have risen above 90% within the black community and the rates of depression, suicide, drug addiction, incarceration, bankruptcy and high school dropout have exponentially increased under strong, totally independent black female leadership.

And though gender separatism has been embraced as the black female concept of genius, in the aftermath of decades of this blasphemous insanity black women have emerged as the most devalued, degraded, demoralized, diseased, deserted, desperate, drugged and suicidally depressed women on the planet and the black family, black business and the black agricultural and industrial base have completely ceased to exist as we once knew them and this book has been composed to explain the completely shocking reasons why this has happened and who is in fact behind it.

As I compose this section of this work, I think of a funny occurrence that I often experienced when I was in my twenties. I'd be sitting at a sushi bar somewhere casually socializing with what was generally a middle aged white woman who was invariably sitting next to me waiting on a takeout order.

As we carried on a bit of completely aimless conversation about everything from the weather to the financial state of the nation when the subject of economics would come up I'd often mention that I often thought about the great depression. A statement to which the women would invariably reply, "How can you possibly think about the great depression when you're only in your twenties?"

And I'd invariably reply, "Because my grandfather never ceased to talk about the various aspects of the struggle that he went through to survive the great depression and how in the wake of the great depression my grandparents started several small practicality based businesses in an attempt to protect themselves financially."

And as a result of having been given all of those years of thorough insight, when the great recession of two thousand eight came around I knew exactly what to expect and exactly what moves to make to protect myself and my family economically and we came through the recession without a single scratch. However, the relevance of this story is that today's young black women absolutely have not been able to deal with the problems of abandonment and suicidal depression that they have been faced with because they absolutely have not been given any insight into the true underlying causes of the total withdrawal from black women that have come to be known as the black girl curse.

It is unfortunate that no matter how many young black women go to jail and the morgue (which young black women are doing at a faster rate than anyone else on the planet) these young women's grandmothers have squarely chosen to either lie to their grand-daughters or to remain absolutely and completely silent and completely refuse to help the young women attempt to navigate their way through this mess and their silence is not motivated by pride or embarrassment, it is solely motivated by their totally unparalleled hideousness and by the fact that they have squarely chosen to completely turn their backs on two to three generations of their daughters just as they squarely chose to turn their backs on their parents and grandparents in the Seventies when all of this strong, totally independent black woman insanity started.

The omen that today's young black women have been subjected to is so intense that even though the young women have done absolutely everything that they can conceivably imagine to change their plight, even going as far as getting involved with other races whom have likewise discarded them, which has resulted in today's black women very swiftly becoming the single largest group of sin-gle mothers of interracial children on the planet, and in the wake of all of this self-analysis there has emerged an extremely heated debate concerning the existence of a "Black Girl Curse" that young black women today are completely unaware in fact does exist and was in fact promised to their grandmothers by their great-grand-mothers in the Seventies and this book has been composed to clearly, correctly and completely inform young black women in particular and young people in general about the tremendous cost, dire consequences and inherent dangers of completely turning one's back on and having absolutely no respect for one's elders as today's black grandmothers chose to do when they were young women.

THE LABOR WARS

FOR ALL PRACTICAL INTENTS and purposes what has come to be known as The Black Girl Curse largely has its beginnings in The French Revolution in the late seventeen hundreds, approximately ninety years prior to blacks being released from slavery. It was at this point that The Women's Movement, which initially emerged from France and then migrated directly to America from Russia's Imperial Capital St. Petersburg with Jewish radicals who were outlawed and exiled fugitives from their own country and several of whom were later exiled from the United States, started to gain real momentum as a direct result of industrialist's desperate need for labor as the world's economies were very swiftly transitioning from agriculturally based economies to heavily industrially based economies.

In this brief chapter I simply want to make the point that it was as much of a fallacy that anyone cared about human rights as it was a fallacy that anyone cared about the rights of women during the emergence of American industrialization. After three hundred years of institutionalized slavery in this country prior to the Civil War, Northerners had not somehow finally come to the grand moral conclusion that slavery was a human injustice and a criminal institution that absolutely had to be stopped.

The truth is that the emergence of industrialization created a dire need for ever-increasingly large amounts of cheap labor which was initially supplied through indentured servitude and labor contracts, which were both forms of legal enslavement of mostly poor whites and white immigrants.

However, as the industrial technology and resultantly the dire need for masses of labor grew ever increasingly greater it eventually yielded The Civil War and mass-immigration, both of which were direct responses to the fact that agriculturally based economies and subsequently slave labor had become obsolete.

At the time, white children as young as four often worked and died under deplorable conditions until child labor was finally officially outlawed in the eighteen thirties. When industrialists no longer had legal access to child labor they were able to very successfully use elements of the women's movement to go after women and convince them that their kitchen wasn't a kitchen, but a prison, that their husband wasn't a husband, but an exploiter, that their children weren't children, but a life sentence and that life wasn't life, but a contest in which women were being left behind – hence today's strong, totally independent, multi-generationally dysfunctional, devalued, depressed, drugged, disposable and ultimately inconceivably irrational women.

These were in fact the beginnings of America's ravenous and completely self-destructive obsession with manpower and masculinization, an obsession that rigidly dictated that men, women and children all be willing, able and fully indoctrinated to function as men. This relentlessly iron willed obsession with manpower would eventually radically redefine the roles of the genders, completely rip apart the American family, totally decimate women's feminine concept of self-worth and eventually precipitate black female radical-feminism and yield the black girl curse.

I think that it's vital to be aware of the fact that if robotic labor had been available in the eighteen hundreds there never would have been an underground railroad and an abolitionist movement to end slavery, nor would there have ever been a progressive movement for the civil rights of women because no one other than slaves and women were concerned with them before the emergence of mechanized industry.

The grim reality of capitalist economies is that capitalism is merely a widely accepted form of ravenous, restless and ultimately completely deadly exploitation in which things absolutely must add up or be removed from the exploitive equation and given this totally incontrovertible fact ethics have never played anything more than a low grade cosmetic role in capitalist politics.

As a matter of fact today, in the wake of ultra-efficient robotic technology, we have evolved to the point where everything is solely being determined by numbers and there are absolutely no morals, scruples or any human factor at all period. We have evolved to the point where what were once human beings have now been reduced to being nothing more than totally expendable assets and liabilities whom are very swiftly becoming obsolete, we are reaching the point where in the mathematics of total efficiency those whom are considered to be unproductive and thusly expendable will inevitably be summarily exterminated.

THE GREAT MIGRATION

IT IS NOT BREAKING news to anyone on Earth that black people haven't exactly been on a nearly half of a millennia joy ride in America. People all over the world are aware that we black Americans along with white Americans and many others including the American Indians have experienced enslavement in America. Fact is, that white people were so good at enslaving us because they had been enslaved themselves and had enslaved each other for Centuries prior to discovering that black slaves were the most durable slave on Earth.

Slaves have been traded since man's emergence and white sex slaves are still being traded back and forth all across the continent of Eurasia at this very moment, so our enslavement in America was not completely unique within the history of the world or the country. However, what in fact has been unique is the slander campaigns that have been waged against black Americans for as long as there has been mass-media, global slander campaigns that have caused narrow minded individuals in virtually every corner of the world to believe that all black people are lazy, irresponsible, dimwitted, totally dependent, socially dysfunctional and completely criminal, while not making mention of the fact that much of the modern world wouldn't be what it is today without black contributions like all forms of mobile refrigeration, 3D computer graphics and numerous other technological advancements of every conceivable kind.

Since the very inception of moving pictures blacks have always been portrayed in a negative stereotypical light often being cast as dimwits and servants and from these slave based sub-cultural portrayals of black people eventually emerged what has come to be known as "The Mammy Archetype." The Mammy Archetype wasn't something that I personally found offensive, but then neither was my beloved "Curious George" the little brown monkey or many other things that have deeply offended many blacks whose sole definition of self is someone who is loathsome and degrading; an unfortunate condition that I have fortunately never suffered.

The Mammy Archetype was basically a largely truth based and entertainment and advertisement propagated cultural ideology that all black women were obese, servile, temperamental and inconceivably dimwitted individuals who were invariably the housemaids of wealthy white families, a very real dimension of American Culture which went on for well in excess of 300 years of American History, and in a desperate attempt to escape "The Mammy Archetype" and all that was considered to be a reminder of their former enslavement many blacks left the Southern States, including millions of black teen single mothers, swearing that they would never return, some didn't even come back South for funerals, Thanksgiving or Christmas.

At the time, the prevailing consensus among Americans in general and blacks in particular was that a much better life and far greater opportunities awaited them in The Great Northern Industrial Centers that were put on the global map by the invention of mass-production that was highly refined and introduced to American Industry by enterprising businessmen like Gustavus Swift and Henry Ford and this firm conviction and the unimpeded lynching of blacks, among a myriad of other factors, precipitated a mass-exodus of blacks from the Southern States.

Even as late as the Eighties people were still talking about the wild rumors of the benefits of moving to places like Chicago that were swirling around in the thirties. These rumors were very entertaining to white people of the time and even today their grandchildren can tell you very entertaining stories of them.

I can remember a funny story that a would-be comedic white trucker once told me about how all of the blacks were convinced to leave Mississippi back in the thirties. According to his entertaining version of the story, huge slaughter houses in Chicago were giving away hog intestines, pig tails and many other pork waste products that Northern whites generally didn't eat but which were the staples of soul food for blacks because on slave plantations waste products were the only food that slaves were given to eat.

According to the gear jamming comedian's version of the story, once word of free access to these pork waste products got around people started calling back down to Mississippi telling their friends, "Girl, they're giving away food up here! You'd better yourself up here to Chicago!"

That, according to his account, is how all of the blacks were convinced to migrate to Chicago. And it doesn't sound far from the truth to me. Whether that entertaining tale was true or not, I don't know, but for a couple of good ol' boys from the Deep South it made for a good hearty laugh.

However, what's even funnier is when I tell Northern white girls, generally teenaged waitresses, the same story.

After I run the whole story down to them I'm like, "Yummmmy, I loves me some chitterlings!"

And the girls are usually like, "Chitterlings?! What on Earth are chitterlings?!"

Then with a great big Cheshire Cat smile I tell them, "Chitterlings my dear, are hog intestines."

And in invariably stunned disbelief they reply, "Hog intestines?! Who on Earth would eat that?!!!"

Then I ask them what they think that hotdogs and bologna are made of and they look like they want to heave.

Then I inform them that pork plants process every part of the pig except the squeal.

Is that wrong?

While I'm on the subject of shock, I can clearly recall my grandfather telling me that he clearly recalled being able to buy buckets of chitterlings for ten cents per bucket and cases of ribs for fifty cents per case back when he started his chain of Bar-B-Q restaurants in Memphis in the mid-thirties. As a matter of fact, I think that the mere thought of paying ten to twelve dollars for buckets of chitterlings and well in excess of fifty five dollars per case for cases of pork ribs are part of what eventually killed him when he died in the mid- Nineties.

However, whatever their true motivations were, Blacks and many other people believed that there was a far better life in the Northern industrial centers and by the time that this migration was finished in the Seventies it had been the greatest willful internal migration in American history which had facilitated the migration of tens of millions and eventually made companies like Greyhound Bus Lines and whoever was selling greasy bags of fried chicken and mason jars of homemade lemonade hundreds of millions of dollars richer. And when the Northern migration finally ended in the late Seventies many companies that had been built on the business provided by the migration soon fell into bankruptcy.

LABOR OUTSOURCING AND THE SUBVERSION OF THE BLACK INDUSTRIAL REVOLUTION

UNTIL THE LATE SEVENTIES, when the black girl curse arose, for nearly the full span of black American history black women had been employed as cooks, maids and nannies and kept as sex slaves, mistresses and even secret wives by white men and everybody else who could access and afford them.

A very strange aspect of our relationship with whites during the Centuries that we have lived with and among them has been that white people have not been able to even think of venturing to any corner of the world without blacks. As a matter of fact, the only place that American whites have ventured to in the absence of blacks is space and they eventually even took us to space with them. Go figure.

Even when blacks were enslaved by whites, it was the most intimate enslavement in recorded history in that children that slave owners had both with their wives and with their slaves all lived and even slept together in the slave owner's residence with the mulatto children often sleeping at the foot of the bed of their white siblings. And in places like the Carolinas some of these mulattos even owned plantations themselves during slavery.

Though many people don't like to hear it, people should be very careful of what happens to black people because in every aspect of life what has effected one group has soon likewise dramatically effected the other. For example, when black farmers started to go bankrupt on a totally unprecedented scale in the Sixties, invariably prejudice and subsequently relentlessly critical of blacks and black businesses, white farmers claimed that black farms were going bankrupt on such an unprecedented scale because negro farmers were dimwits who were lazy and more concerned with whoring around and drinking than they were with farming and niggers were just too ignorant to run and manage a farm or any other business. However, twenty years later when white family farms likewise started to go out of business on a totally unprecedented scale, as opposed to criticism there was Farm Aid, The Agricultural Credit Act and major unfair trade practices lawsuits (which black farmers were cut out of) to help avert the bankruptcy and mass-suicide of what were touted as hard working white farm families who were being preyed upon by big bad bankers when in reality what these invariably racist and totally inconsiderate fucking morons didn't realize was that a general shift in the agricultural industry from small family based farms to large commercial farms, which would bring about exponential increases in both costs and profits, was under way.

This exact same pattern revealed itself again when Crack Cocaine and Crystal Meth hit the U.S. Narcotics Market. If one wishes to truly understand global epidemics of drug addiction, it is first of all extremely vitally important to understand that the flow of drugs into any part of the world is invariably directly parallel to the flow of Indian and Pakistani influence into that same part of the world, whether it be Asia, Afghanistan, North America or South Africa.

When Crack first hit America's streets in the early Eighties and started to ravish black families, black on black crime went right through the ceiling and black family dysfunction and its auxiliaries like street pimping and gangsterdom likewise exponentially increased to the point that they went right through the ceiling. However, it's very interesting that when the black community found itself plagued with a new generation of drugs, whites very quickly claimed that blacks were having problems with crime and drugs because niggers were inherent low-lives and when black thugs started dealing drugs on urban street corners local corner drug stores that had been dealing drugs on the corner for Centuries suddenly became pharmacies instead of corner drug stores as the licensed drug dealers subtly moved to distinguish themselves from the unlicensed.

And ten years later, when rural, as opposed to urban, drug epidemics like Crystal Meth hit rural white communities, instead of it being reported that whites were no good drug addicts, it was reported that America had a drug problem, whereas when drugs were ravishing the black community, it was reported for decades that blacks, as opposed to Americans, had a drug problem.

In the 50s, right after America's victorious emergence from World War II, which saw America set itself up for global economic domination by defeating and creating strategic alliances with what were already its trade partners for more than a Century before the war, America experienced an era of general prosperity and Black America was likewise able to partake in that prosperity as Black Americans had likewise reluctantly taken part in World War II.

At the time there were more black businesses in both the North and the South than there had ever been at any time in American history, slavery had been over for less than one hundred years and under segregation blacks had created a steam roller economy complete with its own university system that was training and educating students from all over the world as non-white university students could only go to colored universities.

As a direct result of all of the aforementioned activity some blacks were very swiftly gaining more wealth and mobility, enough mobility in fact to eventually create a civil rights movement that was far from popular with government and business institutions.

It is an insurmountably morbid fact of life that absolutely no one likes competition, especially not competition that those who are well entrenched in the power structure don't see themselves winning. And the idea of white businesses competing directly with black businesses who had the tremendous advantage of highly motivated former slave labor did not sit well with some people in the establishment and in the aftermath of the eventual civil rights movement, which ultimately precipitated the death of Dr. Martin Luther King Jr. and the violently destructive riots in much of the country that followed Dr. King's assassination in my very own Memphis, Tennessee, a radically militant separatist culture emerged within black communities all across the country.

Many of these militants were racial separatists who had in fact long wanted to fight a bloody civil war with whites and had always viewed men like Dr. King, whom I am absolutely convinced was a federal agent (exactly as it has been revealed that several other key figures of The Civil Rights Movement were) who went bad and eventually became a horribly out of control liability to the government, as government stooges who were merely the black face of the civil rights movement that they were convinced was nothing more than a government ploy to pacify the black community.

Once law enforcement attempted to regain control of American cities in the wake of Dr. King's assassination martial law and a wave of police brutality ensued and the culture of rebellion, spite and rage towards white people grew increasingly more intense within the black community.

Urban black women composed a large portion of this radical movement and as the current of the times became increasingly violent and resultantly increasingly more gangster and separatist so did urban American black women. And as this collective culture of increasing callousness became more and more prevalent urban black women eventually evolved into radical-feminists who felt that they had been wronged and betrayed by everyone and soon urban black women turned their backs on everyone including their own parents.

On the other side of the tracks, as members of the white business establishment observed all of these developments they likewise felt a sense of betrayal and repulsion. They felt that the blacks that they had viewed themselves as having done so much to liberate from the plantations and lynchings and totally unrelenting prejudices and injustices of the South had not appreciated a single bit of their outreach and facilitation.

In the aftermath of black's freedom from agricultural enslavement there had in fact been raging debates over what would become of newly freed blacks. After winning the civil war and having moved in and burned down, bankrupted and completely ravished the Southern slave owners many in the North saw a perfect place for blacks within the laboring ranks of the North's industrial centers. However, though these industrial labor arrangements worked out for a time after the crime waves, riots, drugs, pandering, prostitution and vehement anti-white sentiment the white establishment felt that blacks were inveterate barbarians who wanted too much in exchange for absolutely nothing and they became determined to likewise show their disdain for blacks and black businesses were eventually bankrupted and urban black America was eventually destabilized, collapsed and completely abandoned.

Black businesses were initially crippled by integration which saw countless black consumers flat out abandon black businesses. Then black businesses, and eventually mom and pop sized small businesses in general, were further crippled and finally mortally wounded by the development and institution of the mega market business model in which mega retailers were able to buy products in bulk and resultantly gain huge discounts and offer dramatically lower prices on a level that local retailers nowhere in the country had any hope of competing with; which was in fact very similar to a military tactic designed to exterminate small businesses by the private sector purchasing products on the same scale as the government thereby rendering an urban populace totally dependent on nearly a single source for life sustaining necessities. And today, corner groceries in all areas of the industrialized world have almost been completely replaced with mega-grocers who can buy huge truck, container and ship load quantities of products from foreign countries and resultantly can, and often do, devastate large sectors of businesses and communities.

As the global market started to mature and American businesses became involved in the throws of real global competition American industrial titans were able to exert one of America's primary strengths within the global market place, and that is the totally incomparable ability to access huge resources of low cost labor.

What black slaves had provided in the way of low cost labor to Southern slave owning agriculturalists that had made it possible for them to have a more opulent lifestyle than many European aristocracies, modern industrialists were able to find in third world countries and the result of this was that many of the industrial titans that had provided jobs for urban residents and a huge tax base for local governments packed up and moved offshore leaving many cities bankrupt as they had no tax base in the way of employees or corporations. And since the brothers didn't get the highly controversial forty acres and a mule that was once on the table urban black families had absolutely no access to self-sustaining resources and could not take care of themselves and were resultantly in the position of helpless chicks in the hands of a mighty wolf.

This was the beginning of hyperghettoization, welfare culture and an urban nightmare that would eventually give rise to mass-abandonment, mass-gangsterdom, mass-fratricide, mass-incarceration and the total self-liquidation of Black America's entire agricultural and industrial base of self-sufficiency.

HYPERGHETTOIZATION AND THE DISINTEGRATION OF THE FAMILY UNIT

AN EXTREMELY INTERESTING ASPECT of the collective cultural experience of blacks and whites in America has been our relentless obsession with completely having our way with each-other's women. Given that blacks arrived in America in shackles aboard slave ships white men were very naturally able to freely have their way with black women whom they have used as servants and sex toys for the full span of our American experience. However, black men were initially only able to have, often fatal, encounters with white women that were generally the direct product of either white female curiosity or morbid anxiety at the idea of white men being able to freely have their way with black women while attempting to completely deny white women the freedom to have their way with black men.

In the Northern industrial centers where racial prohibitions were considerably more lax, underworld cultures of black pimps and drug dealers had spent decades pimping on white women, many of whom had been abused by white males and were easily turned into prostitutes who were used as intimate weapons to counter-demoralize and break white men. Before the Sixties this underworld culture was largely overlooked in many parts of the country as many whites felt that any white woman who would get involved with a black man in fact deserved to be pimped.

However, when the collectively irreverent urban culture became completely intolerable white people eventually countered, turned black women into weapons against black men, which caused black women to be discarded exactly as all weapons inevitably are, and then the so-called white squares who supposedly weren't capable of pimping at all, even though they had pimped blacks for three hundred years during slavery, pimped back at the urban black community and released a totally destabilizing barrage of successive waves of everything from a mass-media stigma campaign of relentless slander against blacks to criminal profiling of blacks to blaxploitation cinema to a tsunami of government assistance to a tidal wave of junk drugs to an endless supply of exotic fully automatic weapons and ammunition coupled with the relegation of urban black on black crime investigations to low priority status to anti-child abuse laws that made it possible for children to be forcibly removed from their families by the state to relocation programs to move black women and children to remote states that were far away from their families to high profile campaigns to draft black women into the military to highly abused and ultimately highly division inducing child support laws that precipitated the incarceration of fathers who were delinquent on child support payments while doing absolutely nothing to punish mothers who were denying fathers visitation with their children all of which, combined with a myriad of other hideous tactics, was collectively able to completely destabilize and collapse the black family and eventually destabilized and collapsed the entire American family.

Just as many whites would absolutely refuse to be educated and employed by blacks there has also long been a large part of the black male population that has absolutely refused to be educated and employed by whites. It is not only a religious law but a totally insurmountable pattern of human behavior that those who reject salvation reap wrath. When former black slaves did not appreciate and summarily refused to accept the salvation of modern education and industrialization and instead elected to damn, curse and turn their backs on the white establishment, the white establishment likewise elected to damn, curse and turn its back on the black community.

Though ghettos have existed for millennia, what we have come to know as modern ghettos were in fact invented by the Nazis as staging areas for Jewish captives before they were shipped off to death camps. But why send people to death camps when you can toss in some lead paint and water pipes, industrial pollution, poisoned resources, a few freaked out cops and government policies, a limitless supply of cheap dope and ammunition and let people exterminate themselves.

Recent history has presented the black community with an awesomely stunning array of immoral phenomena that absolutely did not exist and were previously completely unheard of within the black community prior to the mid-nineteen Seventies when feminist black women became totally obsessed with the totally insane idea that they could raise children better all by themselves without men's or their elder's assistance and in the wake of this totally inconceivable blasphemy we have seen the emergence of the consequences of multigenerational family dysfunction that were previously completely unheard of in the black community, such as epidemic suicide, lesbianism, elder abuse, parentally and grand-parentally recommended oral sex, mass-church abandonment and demolition, crimes against clergy, gangster rap, deadly greed and materialism, mass-fratricide, mass-transmission of sexually transmitted diseases, mass-abandonment of women and children at black women's vehement request, total heartlessness like innumerable young mothers dumping newborn infants into garbage dumpsters because they have been convinced by feminists that having a child is going to completely destroy their lives and within the most hideous of ghettos, epidemic torturing of children and even throwing children off of the top of tall buildings.

And in all aforementioned totally incomprehensible cases, one has to seriously ask himself, what in the fuck happened?!!! What precipitated the emergence of this totally incomprehensibly barbaric culture and why do these same patterns keep repeating themselves over and over and over again for what is now going on four generations? Why did all of this start to go right off of the scale in the late Seventies which saw the total disintegration of the black family, black men start to almost exclusively marry white women and black women evolve into straight gangsters whose rate of incarceration managed to increase by 850% between the late Seventies and the new millennia? Why is it that these strong, totally independent black women have now reached the point that black women are now going to prison at a rate that exponentially exceeds that of black men and everyone else on the planet?

The true and correct answer to all of these questions is what has come to be known as "The Black Girl Curse," which is the ominous effects of radical-feminist urban black women abusing, cursing, degrading and summarily dumping absolutely everyone and everything within their circumference, including their own elders and children, and taking tremendous pride in not giving a damn about anything.

I can very clearly recall that in the mid-Seventies when there was an age of insane obsession with progress within urban centers, within the black community we had a catastrophically disastrous situation in which women were running from men, men were running from women and children were running away from home regularly. During that time I lived in the ghettos of Chicago, Illinois with my mother and her generation of inconceivably hideous, profane and ultra-dysfunctional urban black women.

At the time the government was providing low income women with welfare, medic-aide, ultra-low income housing and on the job training in several states, however, as the programs came to be abused by every means imaginable the government instituted regulations that a woman could not receive government assistance if there was a man in the home and the more children that a woman had the more government assistance she was qualified to receive, so what did ingenious black women do? Have as many illegitimate children as they possibly could and turn their backs on everyone and everything that they had ever known in life.

With government backing, which never fails to be inconceivably destructive, black women, like every other group of totally inconceivable morons who has screwed themselves to death with government backing, eventually reached the point that they absolutely could not be told anything by anyone, not even their own parents, grandparents, preachers and teachers and black women eventually began to claim that they were more man than black men and they assured black men that they would never ever chicken-neckin' never need a man of any kind for anything under any circumstances no matter what eventuality presented itself.

Needless to say, at the time this was perceived by black men as the epitome of totally inconceivably blasphemous ignorance and when asked by blacks from outside of America what is wrong with black women my reply is that they are eating too good, and when asked to explain my position I invariably reply that it has been my personal experience that a black woman cannot think on a full stomach but a hungry bitch could run the space program.

By nineteen seventy six, first graders like myself, who were unknowingly the disciples of extremely dark masters of flow, the black religion, were being deeply instilled with firm orders to completely withdraw from black women.

I can very clearly recall that we were told that it was our fault that black women had become so inconceivably impudent and we were told that one of the main reasons that black women were completely out of control was because we had given them far too much attention and in order to solve this problem we were going to have to reverse the flow; which is a very classic black tactic.

One of the firm orders that was issued was to "Let them sit on that ass until it rots if they claim that they'll never need men!" We were instructed that nothing in this life, especially not a woman's ass, had any more value than we gave it, we were likewise instructed that God made man the rib of a woman and if that rib was removed then women would inevitably fold. We were then ordered to completely withdraw our intimacy and support from black women and redirect it to other women while black women, who considered themselves to be smarter than God and their grandparents, were deadly determined to try to defy the structure of the universe and live completely without men.

When black women eventually claimed that they were harder than black men and that black men would need black women long before black women would ever need black men this was taken as a declaration of war by dark masters who devised an array of mortally degenerating tactics to completely diffuse black women of vital energy.

People everywhere on Earth can deal with being attacked by outsiders or traditional enemies, however, the idea of being turned on viciously by your own family sparked unspeakable outrage, especially within the dark religious community. Black women were labeled blasphemers for swearing to be able to defy the very foundation of God's creation and a totally unrelenting religious counter-offensive against them was instituted.

Though women have hung out in temples and churches and tried since the beginning of human history to grasp, comprehend and actually have religion they have invariably failed so black women, even until twenty fourteen, have not realized that they have in fact been involved in a religious counter-offensive; which is invariably the most difficult form of conflict to bring to an end.

At the time there was much talk of a war for souls, which is classic black tactical objective. Black women eventually started to demand that black men get themselves white women because according to black women, white women were weak and needed men where black women were strong and didn't need men of any kind, or anyone else for that matter, for anything, all that black women needed was government assistance to completely revolutionize their lives. Black women claimed that black men were slowing them down and holding them back and if black women could just get rid of their men, parents, preachers and teachers they could take over the entire world all by themselves and more than four decades of totally inconceivable irresponsibility, self-disenfranchisement, totally unparalleled self-destructive insanity and both serially and surreally placing dead last within the black community have proven the results of three entire generations of black women's total inability to figure anything out or think rationally on any level.

People like the Somalians who have just arrived in America and know absolutely nothing about this country or its complex culture often conclude that the government tricked black women into believing that they didn't need men by placing women above men, when in reality the government didn't promise anyone an eternity of government assistance nor did the government instruct three generations of black women to completely turn their backs on God and their grandparents. The government merely facilitated blasphemy and black women reacted as any group of women in the world's history would have. Total dissatisfaction and gross impatience are merely feminine nature, which made welfare like tossing a ball in front of a speeding bus, no matter how many times the ball is tossed, all of the dumb ass kids are going to make a grab for it and get run over.

However, I absolutely must give credit where credit is truly due. Absolutely nobody can deny that The United States Government is a totally unparalleled prodigal genius at creating destabilizing, totally irreconcilable divisions between groups of people and as a direct result of this stunning capability, now, more than thirty five years after the initiation of the totally jackass sisters are doing it for themselves program, the black community has gone through a self-inflicted holocaust and the black community is more divided than we have ever been in our history.

The black community has evolved into such a dysfunctional ultra-subculture in fact that all forms of family, even churches, gangs and prostitution rings have completely disintegrated.

I can remember days not so long ago when black women were so sought after within the black community that they couldn't even walk the streets without someone trying to get their attention or begging them for their time. I can recall a time when black women had overwhelming support and guidance from their men, their parents, their preachers, their teachers and other members of their community. However, today these same inconceivably inconsiderate individuals who sent black men away to white women forever are now grandmothers themselves who are asking all over the black community... "Where are the black men? Why did they drop us, and what is so special about white women?" When these are in fact questions that black women, especially today's black grandmothers, know all too well that they need to be asking themselves. Black women know well that it was in fact black women who declared open season on white women and claimed that black men needed to get going over to Snowville never to return.

At absolutely no point in human history have black men ever put a barrier between themselves and the pussy, it is invariably always women who erect barriers between men and themselves and never cease to complain about men wanting access to women's sexuality to the point that no self-respecting man on the face of the planet would want to be involved with them and they subsequently become self-isolated throwaway women... Which is precisely what has occurred in the case of black women.

I have long said that the worst thing that ever happened to black women in this nation's history is that they were able to get people's attention. When radical-feminist black women determined that they were going to be heard and they got up in every one in America's face and told us all to go straight to hell because they didn't need anyone on the planet for anything and they absolutely assured everyone that they meant what they said and said what they meant their entire existence as a race of women changed. By speaking innumerable blasphemies for decades on end black women cursed themselves as a race of women and from the mid-Seventies forward in every conceivable aspect of American life black women have been replaced with White, Hispanic, Asian and soon Middle Eastern women.

The legions of black nannies that had for Centuries raised generations of white children have all been replaced with Hispanics, the legions of black wives, girlfriends and lovers that had been worshipped by matriarchal black men for the complete length of black history were replaced with white women and the legions of black female guides and confidants were replaced with Asians. None of this would have ever happened if black women hadn't got people's attention and gave people a piece of their warped minds.

Being "The Rationally Challenged" women that nobody can deny that black women are, I would think that instead of trying to give other people a piece of the mind that they obviously didn't have they would have been far better off trying to hold on to what little sense they had. However, since black women weren't able to conclude this, even with the advice of a generation of excellent black grandmothers, they threw away everything including the black church, black agriculture and business and the lives of generations of their children.

If black women had never decided as a race of women that every pussy hungry ass nigger needed to get out of their face and get himself a white woman they would have never ever had a problem and black men would still be chasing black women around licking up to them, appeasing them, begging them for their time and taking great pleasure in flat out kissing black women's big ol' butts just as black men have done for the full span of human history.

I always say that the vagina is a neutralizer and if a woman cannot rub her booty on a problem and solve it then she invariably has no solution. The sexual revolution in this country propagated sex as a form of liberation and the vagina as an object of worship, for black women this was a form of empowerment that proved to be far too much for them to handle as black women eventually came to feel so empowered that they collectively concluded that they would never need anyone for anything.

Common sense would tell anyone who possessed it, that much like gangsterdom, if feminism was supposed to be so beneficial to people in general, as feminists invariably claim that it is, then people would be being benefitted by feminism as opposed to there being a long, bloody trail of epidemic crime, poverty, addiction, suicidal depression and multigenerational family dysfunction all of which has been carried out by the children of strong, totally independent black women who compose in excess of 90% of the North American Prison Population.

Black women love calling black men worthless and irresponsible but it is quite interesting that the level of valuelessness and irresponsibility within the black community has exponentially increased since black women became mortally determined to raise children all by themselves and it is also interesting that black women are likewise being abandoned by every other group of men that gets involved with them, so now we're seeing a generation of single black mothers of interracial children springing up all over the country, proving once again that if you can't work with what you have then you can never work with anything that you ever get in this life.

However, what I find stunning is not the ignorance, what is completely stunning to me is the totally unfailing determination of older women to keep young women as far in the dark as they possibly can about absolutely everything. Though this tremendous faith in darkness is a natural reflex action for women in general, I have always found it to be totally counterproductive to young people.

Young black people, especially young black women, are suffering an inconceivable amount of mental anguish as they try to figure out why it seems that the entire world is against them and these young people deserve answers, and as always they will never ever receive those answers from women because women are completely obsessed with keeping young people in the dark.

As a black man who lived through several of the great social divisions within this country at the very nucleus of their unfolding I am really tired of seeing young black people being baffled by a total lack of knowledge of these important issues that are dramatically affecting their young lives.

I can only wish that our grandmothers and great grandmothers who were born at the turn of the century could have lived to see the inconceivable mess that not heeding their vehement warnings created for their daughters, granddaughters and great-granddaughters. If the black women who are grandmothers today could have listened to their mothers and grandmothers for even a millisecond black women would have never had a problem at all, but I watched myself as today's black grandmothers completely turned their backs on all of their elders when they were young women which has resulted in the situation that black women have today.

Fact is that everything in black women's lives is like a roll of toilet paper that has absolutely no value at all to them until they reach for it and it's not there for them. Everything that black women have is completely valueless to them when they possess it, however, when they inevitably throw it away and someone who actually has values gets that same thing and makes an infinitely better life for themselves the value of that thing is multiplied exponentially in the eyes of black women and black women cannot get beyond this; black women, who have long believed themselves to be exponentially more intelligent than all of their elders, cannot figure their way out of this cycle of self-victimization.

I love to give women an equation that no woman in the world's history has ever been able to figure out, and the equation is $0 - 0 = 0$. Common sense should tell an entire race of women that if everything that you've ever had in life is of tremendous value to everyone except you and people are flooding away from you like crazy and living your dreams with your trash you need to check yourselves. In life we have to learn to be our own best friend as individuals at the very least, because we all have far more potential to do harm to ourselves than anyone else simply because of proximity.

When I was a child urban America was so unspeakably hideous that it was like living within the confines of the psych ward of a gigantic mental institution. Millions of black children all across the country were being mock raised on marijuana and Pink Champale by a generation of black single mothers who have in fact been child, elder and substance abusers all of their lives, abusers who were so inconceivably loathsome that an entire generation of black men is not willing to get involved with anyone who even remotely resembles them as a direct result of being exposed to these women who have managed to become the world's first nearly entire generation of single junky grandmothers.

When individuals become so torn down by others that they begin to tear down, deprive and completely isolate themselves and even burn their own bras and other symbols of their own gender because they believe that other genders and races of people have things better, then they have lost all self-worth and have truly been broken.

When we turn our backs on our own elders who are solely concerned with our own best interests in our relentless pursuit of greed and selfishness we are supposed to suffer.

Waste not want not is cave woman sensibility which has completely ceased to exist within the black female community, the great tragedy of womanhood is that women never figure anything out until it's too late and worse than that no one can tell them anything, not even their own grandmothers, and they are causatively doomed to learn from catastrophic disasters as opposed to casual mistakes.

The real core of the problem is that our obsessive focus on hyper-accelerated progress and numbers is numbing us, tearing us apart and completely destroying our sense of values and the result of our total inability to withdraw from this culture of self-destruction is that we have become a completely valueless society. We have reached the point where there is absolutely no such thing as American family values, we have evolved into a culture in which people take tremendous pride in giving a damn about absolutely nothing.

Over the last few decades wealth in the form of welfare and the divorce lawsuit frenzy has weighed America down and completely demolished American's sense of values as a developing culture, which is very interestingly a direct result of the fact that America is a completely classless society in that given the fact that we don't have an aristocracy we likewise don't have a class system, we have tax brackets, and instead of trying to marry into a higher class women are obsessed with trying to get into a higher tax bracket.

It never fails that extreme wealth completely destroys the life of low class individuals, North America has evolved into an advanced subculture in that today's women don't have the sense that God gave the cave woman and in every corner of society people are coming apart and the continent is becoming fragmented and we are very swiftly losing what has already become our former status as a world leader and innovator as a direct result.

Right now, because of the total lack of family values, The North American Continent is wide open to be conquered by anyone, including our new immigrants from the Middle East.

Right now absolutely anyone in the world can walk right into North America and take over the entire continent in a single generation simply by getting married and having the good sense to have family values. Legions of men in North America would very quickly marry off to any woman or group of women in the world who have this much intelligence because they sure don't exist in North America. And as concrete proof of this there are marriage tours going to every corner of the world where there are not black women and North American men from all races and all walks of life are trying to find sensible, helpful wives who value marriage as a vital institution as opposed to a government sanctioned form of prostitution.

In a nutshell, North American men are in desperate search of women who will assist them in making a bright future for themselves and their family, not a bunch of masculine freakazoids whom they're sure will sue the shit out of them for a fast buck. The point here is ultimately that cultural dysfunction is a cultural problem. However, what's even more ironic than all of the aforementioned madness that surrounds black women, who are solitarily confined prisoners of their own madness, is that being a natural observer of women I'm seeing white women go through the exact same situation that black women have experienced.

While welfare succeeded wildly at corrupting black women and getting three successive generations of black women to completely turn their backs on all of their elders, the culture of divorce for quick and easy profit has done the exact same thing to white women who have likewise turned their backs on all of their elders and the same actions are naturally yielding the same results.

For the last several decades white men have been completely obsessed with out-marrying, for years white men have said that, "No one will ever love you like your mother or fuck you over like your wife!" And they mean it, and they are tired of it. White people have never been big fans of parting with their hard earned cash and this culture of divorce that has become so prevalent in North America has really taken a financial toll on them over the years.

White women, who have been being flat out straight pimped by divorce attorneys who are able to convince them to turn on their husbands for hefty divorce settlements, have reached the point where absolutely no one trusts or can afford them and this has resulted in a mass-exodus away from white women.

Since the Eighties white men have increasingly started to marry Asian women whom, with the exception of Filipinos and Koreans, are the last oasis of family values and feminine sensibility on the planet. As a matter of fact, I was happily married to an Asian woman for twenty three years myself before she succumbed to industrial waste mismanagement induced severe mental illness. And as inconceivably desperate as Western men have become for women who possess even a remote form of sensibility, mark my words, "Pretty soon they'll be pursuing and marrying hijab wearing traditional Islamic women next because eras of total freedom never fail to be followed by some form of religious extremity."

When black women claimed that they were never, ever, chicken-neckin' never going to need men for anything in nineteen seventy five the black family as we once knew it completely ceased to exist. And approximately five years later in the early Eighties when financial advisors started to tell yuppies that the single most potentially devastating threat to their finances was a marriage the white family completely ceased to exist as whites once knew it.

I have long said that there is absolutely no difference between three dimensions of baby mama drama and three ex-wives. I have also long said that the only difference between black women and white women is that black women are completely obsessed with throwing everything that they have away and white women are completely obsessed with taking things from people. However, though these two opposing cultures are quite different from each other they are still equally self-detrimental and detrimental to American society in general.

The point here is that fear and poverty are not circumstances or conditions, but cultures, cultures that are passed on and maintained for generations. You can't send everyone straight to hell and then have them right there to support you when you desperately need assistance. You can't spend the whole of your days being totally mad and then wonder why your entire environment is full of complete madness. The completely insurmountable law of life is that monsters create monsters and they are inevitably devoured by the monsters that they have created.

GANGSTA BITCH SYNDROME

IN THE MID-SEVENTIES OUR grandmothers called all of the aforementioned activity blasphemy, and when I researched the definition of the word blasphemy it was like reading an omen right out of the last Century; the various definitions of the word blasphemy were detailed, completely accurate descriptions of the actions that ultimately precipitated "The Black Girl Curse."

Blaspheme is defined as: Curse, damn, ban, swear, denounce, desecrate, criticize, abuse, lash, rail against, slur, slander, defame, depreciate, mock, scorn and belittle.

Blasphemous is defined as: Sacrilegious, profane, irreverent, unholy, undevout, unsanctified, godless, evil and iniquitous.

Curse is defined as: Profanity, abuse, scourge, oath and excommunication.

Irreverence is defined as: Desecration, disrespectfulness, impudence, insolence, irreligious and sacrilegious.

Sacrilegious is defined as: Blasphemous, profane, disrespectful, desecrative, perverted and corrupt.

Sacrilege is defined as: Lowering, cheapening, abuse, maltreatment, contamination, infection and prostitution.

These words are eerily ominous and extremely accurate descriptions of the lifestyle and culture of inconceivably profane and unscrupulous urban radical-feminist so called strong, totally independent black women whose extremely warped concepts of strength and masculinity were eventually glorified by mass-media through everything from the media's beloved bad news about the black community to blaxploitation cinema into the sole definition of black women and this culture of living life on a gang war footing where everything is solely measured in terms of strength and weakness, where every completely inexcusably outrageous and hideous act is blamed on survival and in order to be viewed as a strong, totally independent black woman a woman has to be totally prepared to raise her children all by herself and deal with a myriad of harsh realities.

It is precisely this kind of lifestyle of feminine gangsterdom that ultimately spawned what has come to be known as "Mangina Culture" that has eventually been able to completely high jack black female identity and culture to the point that today it has in fact become the dominant black female identity and culture and after what is now going on four generations of this "Mangina Culture" black women cannot think, act or function outside of it. And as a direct result, today black women from all walks of life firmly believe that men don't want to be involved with black women because they are so strong that they cannot be controlled like other women, when in fact there are other women who possess characteristics like sensibility and family values that men who don't want women who have to be controlled by other people are very attracted to; women whom the manginas of this world would invariably view as submissive and weak which is straight gangster mentality.

And this, people, is in fact the nucleus of what has come to be known as "The Black Girl Curse" which is in core essence a multi-faceted hyper-acceleration based psychological viral epidemic that is the morbid product of several factors including ideals of total freedom, total independence, total self-determination, gender supremacy, role reversal, extremely warped concepts of strength and masculinity and gangster mentality all of which combined have yielded Gangsta Bitch Syndrome which has very effectively resulted in what is now four generations of urban black women becoming the most masculine women on the face of the Earth and subsequently choosing to completely turn their backs on all of their elders, the church, their men, and black business and choosing to literally sell their souls and abandon their entire support base in exchange for drugs, discos, dog tracks and a tsunami of loans, grants, and other forms of government assistance.

There has in fact never even remotely been more epidemic crime, irresponsibility, multi-generational family dysfunction, depression, drug addiction, mass-fratricide, mass-incarceration and mass-liquidation of the agricultural and industrial base within the black community than there has been since strong, totally independent, self-isolationist throwaway women have become obsessed with being female heads of household.

It is important to be aware of the fact that, what we have come to know as The Women's Movement is Centuries old and in fact got its start in France due to the fact that France is also the birth place of The Industrial Revolution which subsequently spawned The French Revolution.

While French Commoners were fighting for labor rights and attempting to break free from The French Aristocracy, in their desperation for support they attempted to gain the support of women, whom were initially what has come to be termed Equality Feminists who wanted the right to vote, the right to land ownership, the right to own businesses, the right of self-determination without the signature of their father, etc. and since men were engaged in a general revolution that aimed for reformation of legal rights, women also revolted along with the men and appended their fight for women's rights to the general revolution that was taking place at the time. This pattern also repeated itself in Switzerland, Germany and eventually on a grand scale in Russia during the Russian Revolution from which America directly inherited its women's movement when Russian Feminists were outlawed and expelled from Russia during The Bloody Bolshevik Revolution.

In feminism's Centuries old history, it is something that has not been one dimensional, there have in fact been two basic tiers of feminism, Upper Tier Equality Feminism and Lower Tier Gender Separatist Radical-feminism, which have both grown and evolved in direct parallel to each other and can no more be separated from each other than an Aristocratic Field Marshal can be separated from the murderers and rapists that serve beneath him under his direct command.

A dark fact of The Women's Movement that has always gone completely unacknowledged is that, many of feminism's original and most tireless, loyal and highly dedicated financers and supporters have long been prostitutes whom, right from the beginning, have been radical-feminists who have long viewed marriage as a form of exploitation, a family as a form of enslavement and a husband as a government sanctioned exploiter of women.

This is in fact why L' Oriel, which got its start as a German immigrant founded chemical research and development corporation, and many other global clothiers and cosmetics companies got their start in France, because given that common women didn't have the disposable income to spend on fashion and cosmetics and engage in aristocratic dressing, hair dressing and cosmetic rituals like The Elaborate French Dressing Ritual of Toilette, the only support base that French Clothiers and Cosmetics Manufacturers had was the Female Aristocracy.

However, as the aristocracy began to be collapsed by revolutionaries, including highly ambitious industrialists, feminists and radical-feminists, the only women that French Clothiers and Cosmetics manufacturers had to turn to for survival and the aspiring global expansion of their consumer base were prostitutes, because prostitutes were the only women who had disposable income to spend on such things freely without their father or husband's permission.

Even today, France has as a huge, deeply ingrained culture of politically active prostitutes whom have engaged in politics for Centuries and whom French Industrialists, militarists, revolutionaries and feminists in fact owe a tremendous debt of gratitude. However, my Grand Inquisitor Level Pimpnological Conclusion on feminism is that it is in fact a highly elaborate con.

While I absolutely am not against the ideals of freedom and equality, historically, there have been direct parallels between exploitation, militarism, feminism, prostitution and homosexuality, all of which are dimensions of extremism that are intertwined and both invariably and inveterately conjure one another, coexist and function in tandem and given the fact that feminism ultimately has its roots in militarism and industrial exploitation and the fact that women can never ever be satisfied with anything, combined with the totally insurmountable fact that militant Coup D'etats that seek to install inherently destructive militants (including feminists) in administrative positions invariably don't work.

If feminists, and women in general, were really all about equality, mutual respect and the betterment of humanity, people would in fact be being bettered as opposed to increasingly highly armed and sorely embittered. However, since drama, disrespect and total dissatisfaction are what women are ultimately all about, drama, dissatisfaction, social dysfunction, gender separatism, a growing culture of concealed weaponry and deadly domestic conflict and an ever increasingly grossly over-complicated legal landscape, in which even children have come to be mass-incarcerated, are all that have emerged from modern women's ravenous obsession with total self-isolation and morbid radical-feminism.

At its core, feminism is ultimately a grand exercise in futility that has in fact been mortally detrimental to all forms of both family and surrogate family (which are the core vital units of any society) which have quite literally been poisoned to death and sequentially families have been poisoned to death, which has seen an exponential increase in the divorce rate, which has increased by 90% within The Black Community since The Sixties, surrogate families have been poisoned to death, which has seen an exponential decrease in gang, prostitution ring, masonic organization and military and police recruitment and membership.

Even homosexual couples are experiencing exponential rates of relationship dysfunction and even after Centuries of continual engagement in all forms of feminist activity women continuously claim that they are still treated as second class citizens by men, that they have much more to accomplish and women are generally completely dissatisfied with the level of equality that has been accomplished over the Centuries of feminism's existence.

Since the Sixties, blacks haven't had a private sector and subsequently the private sector investment that we once had in the black community when we had an expanding agricultural and industrial base in the Thirties, Forties and Fifties and subsequently strong, totally independent gangsta bitch strongholds like New York, Chicago, Detroit, Baltimore, St. Louis and Atlanta have suffered tremendous urban decay.

Just as gangsters sell protectionism as a lame excuse for their invariably ass-backward, half sideways and totally self-destructive existence, gangsta bitches, who are invariably the single mothers of gangsters, have likewise sold totally inconceivable morons extremely warped concepts of black female strength and masculinity that have yielded the total collapse of all of the economic invention and subsequent socio-economic gains that blacks have made since our release from slavery in the 1860s and this Gangsta Bitch Syndrome is in fact an exponentially deadly destructive multi-generational psychological viral epidemic within the black community (just as ultra-nationalism and white supremacy were exponentially deadly destructive multi-generational psychological viruses within the European Community prior to World War II) among willfully self-detrimental, omni-dysfunctional, abusive, offensive and awe-inspiringly ass-backward and half-sideways thinking individuals who very loudly and proudly refer to themselves as strong, totally independent black women who have in fact become like the Ku Klux Klan in that they can't get anyone who knows anything about them to get involved with them.

Today's post major government assistance era chicken-heads / project chicks, who have in the past few decades very loudly and proudly termed themselves Ghetto Queens, who have ironically had The United States Government finance every conceivable aspect of their lives for the full span of their lives, have in fact reached the point where they have basically branched off into two equally self-detrimental extremist groups; one group consisting of totally independent hyperghettoized federal prison bound bone thug mangina type hard core lesbian radical-feminist gangster bitches and the other group consisting of highly indoctrinated and ultra-dysfunctional, "If it's white it's right!," hard core white supremacists who in fact have more faith in white people than white people have in themselves.

The so-called strong, totally independent black women of today have absolutely no idea that long before the great migration, hyper-urbanization and hyperghettoization the real original reason that black women in fact came to be known and extremely highly respected as strong black women was not because they didn't have any respect for anyone or anything, but because during slavery if black women were pregnant they had to have their babies in the field all by themselves and wrap their babies up and keep working or be severely beaten.

For four Centuries American black women were ultra-functional and they were resultantly completely taking care of both their own families and the families of their masters. This culture continued well into the nineteen Seventies in urban centers and well into the Eighties in parts of the Deep South.

Pre-nineteen Seventies black children were so well disciplined that black women were able to control their children merely by giving them stern, disapproving looks that signaled that someone was going to get hurt for doing something that they weren't supposed to be doing and then they were going to get hurt again if their father found out that they had given their mother any trouble, so black children came to be known as model disciplined children.

The aforementioned strong black woman was never a problem within the black community, however, "The so-called strong, totally independent black women" that were born in the fifties and emerged on the streets between nineteen sixty five and nineteen eighty after having completely turned their back on the strong black woman and dumping the black family in exchange for welfare and radical-feminism were a totally catastrophic disaster within the black community that have managed to become our first entire generation of single grandparents.

In the mid-seventies, the average black grandparent had the equivalent of a fifth grade education and behind government booster shots, laws and other government programs that resulted in the state replacing people's parents, {which has yielded an effective culture of stranger worship and a love affair with total ignorance in which, especially young women, became far more willing to listen to absolute and complete strangers than they were willing to listen to their own parents whom they had in fact come to believe were stupid because they had a lower numerical grade of education than their children did, even though they in fact lived much longer, had a far better quality of life, had far more real sensibility, generally had far more functional relationships and built and provided exponentially more for the black community than their children who were born in the forties and fifties ever did} black women completely turned their back on God and their grandparents which compelled my grandparents to have an elders meeting in the Eighties in which they collectively concluded that something was perilously wrong within society in general and that what the teachers were teaching the young people at school was wrong and was completely destroying marriages, families and communities and was turning their children into people that they didn't recognize.

Following the huge surges in government assistance and tremendous increases in minority focused special interest programs like "On The Job Training" and "Preferred female military recruiting," in their minds highly educated urban black women completely turned their back on all of their elders and what has ensued in their blasphemously impudent wake has been far worse than taking nose-candy from strangers.

Being a point blank on-site witness to the regressive insanity of black female baby boomers in The Seventies is something that I can only liken to witnessing something as colossal as The Great Pyramids of Egypt making a counter-clockwise rotational shift that no one had the power to turn back to their former logical position.

When one looks at the present state of black women today it is very clear that what black women are suffering is in fact an omen, a very necessant black girl curse that could have very easily been avoided if the black women who are grandmothers today could have heeded the warnings of their elders when they were young women. However, just as they did not heed their elder's vehement warnings they are continuing to lie, deny and leave young black women to suffer in the dark all by themselves without any clue of what they are suffering from or why they have been made to suffer it; real strong black women absolutely would not do this.

Total independence was supposed to be the master key to the black woman's future, however now, every time that you turn on the television you have these mortally depressed junkies on television crying about how they're unloved and unwanted, how they haven't been on a date in years and how they can't find men who are low enough to get involved with them, not to mention marry and stay with them. And when I see all of this slobbering ridiculousness, before I switch the channel all that I want to know is, what part of the master plan was that?

All of this is in fact what initiated and has sustained the culture of total abandonment of black women for half of a Century, not our experience of slavery or some other bullshit that has been theorized by pipe smoking idiots and it is this mortal obsession with a vain culture of multi-generational self-detriment that has made generations of black women insanely determined to continue their endurance of this abandonment which they themselves, not black men, who would never put a barrier between themselves and the pussy, initiated because in that hideous junk yard that is the black female mind they really and truly think that they are strong, totally independent black women which they have been made to believe is something to be extremely proud of for multiple highly self-detrimental generations.

On the extremely rare occasion that I discuss black female blasphemy with other masters I always make the point that women were not put here to hurt people and when they try to hurt people, as I have seen black women try their best do all of my life, they invariably hurt themselves a hundred thousand times worse.

What the strong, totally independent and ingenious sistas have never been able to figure out for the full span of human history is that there are basically only two things in life, balance and collapse, and in the absence of balance all that is left is collapse.

Men build things and women preserve things and in the complete absence of this age-old commonsensical insight, as is invariably the case when children are mock raised by absolutely and completely worthless people who take tremendous pride in giving a damn about absolutely nothing, there is inevitably total destabilization, collapse and the emergence of a total lack of values.

It should be common sense to absolutely anyone who has a functioning brain in their head that you can't throw away everything and have everything at the same time, people can't give other people what they don't have like morals, scruples, respect, self-worth, foresight, a work ethic, etc.

REPRISE OF THE SOUTHERN SEWAGE

THE POINT OF THIS book thus far has ultimately been that, people cry for what they don't have and women ultimately do so much crying for respect because they ultimately don't have genuine respect for other people and subsequently when communities are run solely by women they very quickly degenerate into a state of disrespect, disrepair, irreverence, irresponsibility, self-loathing, self-degradation, self-disenfranchisement and perpetually sustained regression.

Over the years, decades in fact, that I have been observing women, I have found that, much like the pimps that are solely influenced by them, women have the power to accomplish anything in this world that they can push other people to do, however, if they have to do things themselves, that shit simply does not get done... And given this fact, even after half of a Century of consumate failure and catastrophically disastrous results under the control of Black Women, it has never even remotely entered the minds of these awe-inspiringly loathsome and self-detrimental so-called strong, totally independent black women that there has never been more disrespect for women than there has been since women became totally obsessed with raising children all by themselves which has in fact seen the black life span go from an average of 85 years old in The Sixties to being plunged back down to a pre-civil war slave average lifespan of 22 ~ 30 years old for young people by the Eighties and a sustained average age of 60 years old for today's black senior citizens who are living 25% ~ 75% shorter lives. And even though women like to vehemently claim that they care far more about children than men, it is very interesting to me that since women have become mortally obsessed with the radical-feminist insanity of raising children all by themselves juvenile detention centers, prisons, morgues and cemeteries have become perilously overbooked as they have been filled absolutely and completely beyond capacity with multiple generations of the children of strong, totally independent black women. However, women in general are still totally convinced that what they are doing is absolutely ingenious and all of the invariably urban insanity is everybody's fault but their own and very interestingly, instead of being able to figure out that they're doing something wrong, especially black women believe that the more miserable, resource deficient, dependent, disenfranchised, impoverished and threatened they become they are just becoming stronger and stronger.

When The Great Migration started in around nineteen fourteen, many black people who left the Deep South swore that they would never, ever, ever return to the South under any circumstances. However, after migrating North and creating gang, drug and welfare culture and a heritage of totally incontestable blasphemy as well as carrying out a self-inflicted holocaust, precipitating the total disintegration of the black family and totally liquidating the black agricultural and industrial base to the point that they have completely ceased to exist, all of these awe-inspiringly self-disenfranchised low-lives that were supposed to have been raised better by strong, totally independent ghetto trash black women are flooding back into the Deep South which has resulted in cities like Memphis becoming globally recognized as a totally out of control crime center and nationally recognized as The Dirtiest City In The Country and it has likewise resulted in The Southern States having the most overcrowded prisons in The Western Hemisphere.

REVELATION OF THE BRAHMAN MENACE

THANKS TO THOSE INDEFATIGABLY relentless figures that control the global media, which has been described by analytical geniuses as being in the business of spreading darkness at the speed of light, it is clear to absolutely everyone on the face of the Earth that blacks in fact do have a real problem and many people, including non-blacks, have a real interest in understanding the precise cause of that problem which has seen the total disintegration of the black man and the black woman, the black family, the black industrial base and even the black church has ceased to be the rock and the strength of the black community that it once was and has seen the rise of crimes against clergy.

Yes, blacks truly do have a really serious problem, and as a grand inquisitor level criminal profiler, a grand inquisitor level theologian lineage master pimpnological decryptologist, a ten toes stomp down disciple of theologian lineage masters of the true core internal dynamics of total damnation and a star student of both Back Street University and The College of Pimp Knowledge, it is crystal clear to me precisely what the true source of that problem is.

For those grand inquisitor level masters of exploitation and the true core internal dynamics of behavioral dysfunction whom as an ancient culture have collectively taken ages to dissect and occasionally profit immensely from the human circumstantial anomaly of the relentless frequency of black failure and suffering and pass our findings on to our most loyal and inconceivably dedicated disciples whom have in turn continually analyzed our collective findings at all levels, it has become incontrovertibly clear to higher level masters like myself that two of the core causes of black people's sufferings are that we have an age-old thug problem and we have consistently refused to get with the program on any level.

In grim reality, the true root cause of our relentless suffering is the researchable and totally incontrovertible fact that we have not had a problem with any ordinary thugs ravishing, demoralizing, dividing and inconceivably embarrassing our communities all over the planet, we have in fact had an ancient and highly evolved far beyond the furthest stretches of our collective imagination Phantom Menace Thug Problem, an ancient Phantom Menace Thug Problem that evolved from the fact that innumerable millennia ago several extremely radical solutions to an age-old problem were devised which have immersed, not only Blacks and Asians but, the whole of global humanity into a multi-civilizational age of relentless human misery in the interest of global conquest, which is an age-old objective that has haunted man since the beginnings of our residency on this planet.

This Deity Level Phantom Menace Thug Problem has evolved from elements of the Brahman Culture of India, which is in fact the nation of origin of the word thug and a nation that has been genealogically proven to be a repetitively **exiled** wayward child of Africa with a long history of menacing the peoples of its own region and Africans alike and a long and extremely infuriating history of expulsion from the African Continent, the last major **expulsion** having been from the Nation of Uganda by the late, great Idi Amin who claimed to have had a grand premonition that Indians and Jews (ancient bedfellows who are bound by oaths of loyalty as Indian Masters and Jewish disciples for innumerable millennia) were strangling the progress of his nation and its economy so he **expelled** both of them together from The Nation of Uganda and many fled the African Continent altogether (**again**) exactly as has happened many times in the past. And herein lies the core of the true root cause of black misery and suffering, a classic military campaign to gain control of the high ground of The African Continent, which there are no records of ever having been submerged below sea level, which has subsequently resulted in The African Continent continually being under siege by India and further subsequent Indian media mogul induced relentless hatred of Blacks.

The fact that the omni-dimensional and relentlessly aggressive culture that underlies the whole of everything that we can even remotely begin to conceive of as modern civilization has been indefatigably obsessed with gaining control of the entire planet and it is only the continent of Africa that has continually hampered their efforts to accomplish this ancient objective.

Since the most ancient times humanity has been mind-numbingly obsessed with a single objective, Complete Control of humanity and subsequent Conquest of the entirety of the planet and there is absolutely no question in my mind that all of the madness that humanity has long experienced, which continues as a relentless succession of wars and battles that includes every global and imperial war in known history, in fact started in Africa during a time when the Earth was known as Asiyah and all Earthlings were what have come to be known of today as Asians. However, it is clear to me that, just as in all vacuums of power, someone strongly disagreed over whether humanity should be allowed to live freely or whether all men and the entire planet should be conquered and those whom fiercely believed that the entire world and all of humanity should be controlled and conquered were expelled from The African Continent and became what we know of today as Indians.

Indians have the full spectrum of blackness from mustard greens to cannabis to highly capable indigenous cultures of pimps to lions to elephants to African genetic markers and would have absolutely no culture if African influence was removed from them. Since ancient times these Indians have come to refer to the Earth as Bharat Varsha, which is ruled through a militant form of flow known as the Mahabharata which is the longest, most ancient and one of the most powerful poems on the planet.

The totally irrefutable and insurmountable nature of trouble is that when one is having totally inconceivable amounts of long term sustained trouble, that trouble is invariably coming from someone just like themselves, and in the case of Africans, it is in fact other Africans, namely Ethiopians, who have broken away from the African Continent, evolved into Indians, and come to refer to themselves as Brown People instead of Black People.

Historically, all forms of enslavement and widely and extremely genocidal violence have invariably evolved around Empires attempting to reclaim the former boundaries of ancient, long extinct Kingdoms or just flat out making claims that their group is superior to the rest of the world and is thusly God ordained to rule over the rest of humanity and Indians have long covertly done this and referred to India as Bharat Ganaranjya which Indians believe is the center of the world.

Since these Brahmans have not been able to gain any inroads into sustained conquest of either Africa or Eurasia (both of which Indians claim were once colonies of India) for millennia, among the incalculable array of hideous tactics that they have used to attempt to accomplish total conquest of the two Continents, they have opted to use their carefully cultivated and highly evolved satellites like The United States of America and the entirety of Europe, both of whom have absolutely no culture, language, mathematics, religion or ideology of any kind that have not evolved directly from ancient Sanskrit based culture and directly out of the aforementioned Mahabharata (which, in terms of judgments, prejudices, recommended behavioral patterns and rituals, especially of marriage, both the uniquely Asian and precisely Indian Holy Koran and Holy Bible are byproducts) to demoralize, disease, poison, in-debt and enslave their way into control of the African and Eurasian Continents with the use of stooges from the Brahman's European satellites whom have, among other things, been able to collect slaves from the edges of West Africa and very successfully do virtually all of the Brahman's dirty work while The

Brahman Menace is able to remain safely anonymous from all but the ultra-enlightened and continue to wage their campaign of relentless obsession with complete global conquest in complete anonymity.

For those of you who are not truly familiar with the true nature of ancient clandestine cultures of totally inconceivable guerilla extremists and the common patterns of pimps, thugs and other militant extremists it's extremely important to be aware of the fact that a battle can be waged anywhere from a few minutes to a few months, however, wars can be waged for innumerable millennia, encompass several generations and span multiple human civilizations.

Being aware of the fact that power corrupts and complete power corrupts completely one has to ask himself, if you had a totally inexhaustible cache of weapons and tactics how far would you go to accomplish an objective that you were truly dedicated to accomplishing, how many generations would you exterminate, how many nations would you completely wipe off of the face of this Earth, how many civilizations would you completely annihilate, how many millennia would you lay siege to an objective that you were totally dedicated to accomplishing?

The Brahman's sadistic answers to these questions are in fact what lie at the core of The Brahman Aristocracy and the specter of global terrorism on all conceivable, and several totally inconceivable, levels. The aforementioned solutions to long thought to be totally irresolvable military issues that have been devised and perfected by The Brahman Aristocracy are the ability to infinitely sustain a multi-front war for innumerable millennia by fighting on several seemingly unrelated fronts and by hiding mission control behind several layers of operatives whose missions are so top secret that they can't determine or question the true source of the directives that they are acting under and the yield is satellite nations attacking the Brahman's traditional enemies which appear to be very random targets to anyone who is not able to see clear through organizations and get a clear make on what's going on and has the ability to accurately assess who could be doing it.

Anyone who thinks that this kind of thing cannot possibly happen desperately needs to have their head examined, military organizations all over the world have operational planners who have devised finished plans for all kinds of operations, some of which are so radical that they remain indefinitely shelved, the only difference with these Brahmans is that instead of shelving their radical plans for global conquest they have put them into action and kept them in action by employing the use of clandestine religions and organizations, former covert operative military dictators, puppet states and satellite nations that Brahmans have covertly erected from the bottom up.

These people have been conducting these kinds of operations for so long that they have become totally unparalleled masters of having their secret organizational operatives infiltrate national governments, move into positions of power and completely rearrange the given governments academic and legal infrastructure so that when ordered the operatives of age-old secret organizations can precipitate a state of emergence that effectively neutralizes the given government and Brahman mission control can issue directives that aim that nation's resources directly at a targeted entity and the yield is what externally appears to be a completely unwarranted attack against an illogical target like Afghanistan or Vietnam that is in fact one of the Brahman's former territories, traditional enemies or tactical objectives and this, likewise age-old, total lack of genuine sovereignty of leaders of industrialized nations is in fact the real danger that keeps the world hopelessly locked into a cycle of apparently endless global conflict.

As a completely infiltrated state America is a really slick plan, it's not merely a random mistake that America is a huge melting pot that has slaves and refugees from every conceivable corner of the world that yields several behavioral anomalies that would be totally impossible on the same scale in a more culturally refined nation.

Our women's rights / feminism movement, for example, women wanting to have equal rights in virtually any other corner of the world would merely yield a few organizations being established to put pressure on the government to improve disputed gender issues and other situations. However, in America, the yield has been generations of total idiots completely turning their backs on their elders, their elders ancient insights and their indigenous languages to the point that families don't function, children don't have the guidance or discipline to want an education and the nation is inevitably reduced to a state that survival, not to mention success, has become a sensibility contest in which the only functional people left in the country just happen to be Indians who set up the entire dysfunctional mess in the first place precisely per the schedule that has been set by the closely followed chart of the Yugas which designates four Yugas (ages) of which we are now in the Kali Yuga (iron / final/ Armageddon age) which is a Yuga in which righteousness is to be reduced by 75% and while the entire nation is floundering in dysfunction, exactly as is the common pattern during a major pivotal shift, Indians are able to flood into the country and slip right past you (without making eye contact) to observe, record, mark off and supervise the shift.

This is a uniquely Brahman Aristocratic form of prejudice that propagates that lower castes have no ability to run a stable society and if one looks at global history, a single totally anonymous culture has been circumnavigating the globe for innumerable millennia covertly teaching, starting wars, creating deadly epidemics and toppling governments.

This is in fact why there is a constant drift toward one world government and it is likewise precisely why things like The Mysterious Phantom War on Terrorism, which has seen the modern military anomaly of a ground force of comparatively primitive, largely illiterate guerilla units fend off major global superpowers, has been drawn out longer and at a far greater cost than World War II, because The Brahman Menace, this

time under the guise of undefeatable Pakistani Seasonal Fight-
ers, is in fact behind the so-called terrorist organizations and
it is using multiple human extinctions worth of military tactical insight to tactically advise the guerillas on how to fend
off the major global superpowers which the Brahman Menace
itself created and in so doing it is able to fight a multiple front
war from both sides while maintaining complete control of
both ends of the conflict and subsequently very highly effectively and efficiently further progress its influence in, control
over and conquest of the world... One of the primary reasons
that we live in a state of ceaseless global conflict is that, having
realized many human extinctions ago that war is ultimately a
fusion and not a clash, The Brahman Menace is very cunningly
using its many religious and heavy industrial satellites to engage
in ceaseless warfare to literally fuse the entire world together
through ceaseless engagement in warfare and eventually gain
complete control of it. This is in fact some of the most highly
classified top secret information on the planet.

It took me decades of largely unintentional subconscious con-
sideration of the uncommonly high frequency of Brahman on-site
appearance at major pivot points in global history to provide
highly skilled pinpoint precise support and tactical advice to crack
this case. Pivotal points such as The Brahman on-site appearance
during the American Civil Rights Era to directly advise Dr. Martin
Luther King Junior and the Hippy Movement and in South Africa
to advise Nelson Mandela during The South African Civil Rights
movement which saw The Apartheid Menace, whom highly complex racists like Gandhi also supported, deposed and completely
collapsed, just to name a few frequencies of Brahman intervention
into global geopolitics.

I was able to recognize The Brahman Phantom Menace
because as completely Omni-dimensional Global Guerilla Pimps
Indians employ many high level clandestine pimp tactics that are
solely and very uniquely employed by pimps and are thusly easily

recognizable to true master black pimps, signature pimp tactics such as isolating individuals, indirectly threatening and enslaving individuals with religion and making people completely turn their back on everyone that they have ever known and valued in life to tirelessly serve their clandestine lineage pimp masters.

Those of you who are not lineage master products of the black pimp culture are naturally completely unaware of black pimp's life-style, mission, directives and core primary objectives so I'm sure that you will find it completely interesting to become aware that a pimp is in fact an individual who is mind-numbingly obsessed with the development of mind (as opposed to solely brain) power, the development of total self-control and the eventual accomplishment of complete control.

True master pimps are likewise obsessed with the cultivation of the ability to effectively gain or win the soul of someone who has been effectively programmed to give their life for a master pimp if instructed. And in this interest, in solid state traditional pimp cultures we are constantly trained, lectured, observed, quizzed, questioned and by other means tested by our more senior masters, who are absolutely nothing less than gods to us, to assure that our insights and capabilities are being passed and maintained correctly…this is in fact how I discovered the Brahman Menace.

I have always possessed an innate curiosity about how things work and I virtually lived at the Memphis Public Library when I was a teenager and during this time, at about the age of thir-teen, while relentlessly studying the history of The Nazi Menace I noticed that during The Weimar Republic Era there was a very mysterious and obviously clandestine (as they constantly took pho-tographs that conveyed messages by their sitting or standing position and likewise by the way that their heads were positioned) Jewish Brahman Aristocracy that existed who were the wealthiest, most influential and envied people in Weimar Era Germany who were on-site managing the rise of modern Technical and Industrial Ger-many which eventually evolved into the highly Indian influenced

Nazi Menace that eventually evolved into what we now know as the **military-indus**trial complex that through hyper-industrialization very swiftly grew into the vicious beast that devoured slavery, mechanized mass-murder and now travels the world creating problems and selling solutions by developing, financing and training dictators and military juntas and then turning on them and accusing them of being a problem and then going in and demolishing their country and rebuilding them as trade partners, tactics which are an extremely effective spearhead for Brahmanist aggression that is a natural extension of the mass-production of products and the incessantly desperate scrambling for markets on which to sell them that inevitably leads to global military aggression and it is very interesting to me that if you look into the history of **Indus Valley Civilization**, every civilization that has ever been built on the Indus Valley Civilizational model has always been completely wiped out behind sinister business dealings.

I likewise found it interesting that these so-called Brahman Jews were clearly from India…a realization that was strange to me at the time, however, I was a thirteen year old child who was at that point living a normal thirteen year old child's life (aside from having been a lineage disciple of true master pimps since the age of eleven) and these findings were nothing more than a passive interest. However, what was of interest, was the fact that these people were accused of taking over Germany's economy and financially raping and bankrupting the German people with runaway inflation by radical Germans…hence, the Holocaust as a radical solution for the German people to regain control of the country and its economy.

These random findings during my youthful ramblings in the public library would never have caused me to look further into them at that point except for the fact that upon the breaking of the news stories of an Indian cult leader named the Rajneesh in the early Eighties, my attention was effectively directly turned toward this individual by my masters both pimpnological and random predatory master alike, all of whom, without knowing or consulting each other, unanimously concluded that this Rajneesh character was in fact a master pimp, for me this was extremely pivotal and had to be analyzed further and more deeply if I was to ever hope to become an accomplished master pimp.

I can very clearly recall numerous masters laughing about how this Rajneesh character had a cult and one hundred Rolls Royces, which I found impressive at the time, only later did I discover that his female cult members also wore red dresses and other signature pimp cultural patterns that would have made it far beyond obvious to all of my masters that this Indian was in fact an accomplished master pimp, all that I knew was that if my masters all concluded the same thing without consulting each other, then to me it was as good as the word of God.

I think that it is also vital to point out that during that same period our Christian ministers were all preaching very intense sermons about us being caught up in the midst of an extremely intense war for souls (which would fit perfectly with a grand quest for total power that has been initiated, managed and relentlessly carried out by priests) in that a new generation of drugs were pouring into our communities.

Both Europe and America's obsession with prescription and eventually street level drugs has always been directly parallel to the influx of Indians in that, drug use in Europe dramatically increased as levels of wealth, disposable income and disposable time dramatically increased along with the expansion of Europe's Industrial Revolution and North America's drug use dramatically increased in direct parallel to its embracing of Indian Psychedelic Culture that came along with the huge influxes of Indians that poured into North America in the 60s during the Civil Rights Movement, just as Indians were behind the flow of opium and later heroin, which financed the entire Asian Theater of world War II, onto The Asian Continent, specifically into Mainland China and Japan before, during and long after World War II.

To the complete abhorrence of our grandmothers, inconceivably hideous black female radical-feminism was likewise swiftly expanding within the urban black community. Our pimp masters totally protected their disciples from these potentially deadly threats by giving us extremely stern laws and directives to live by which if followed to the letter would neutralize us from the effects of a drug and radical-feminism epidemic and being as insanely dedicated as I was I couldn't have been immunized more effectively if I had been given a series of shots.

It is likewise extremely interesting to note that when the Rajneesh died in 1990 he was rumored to have become a drug addict who was rumored to have been poisoned to death which, just like the death of Michael Jackson, who was likewise continually pointed out by my pimpnological masters as a pimp, was a common undisciplined pimp death pattern. And exactly as is the Indian pattern on the African Continent, Pimp Rajneesh was eventually **exiled** from America in the Eighties in a political influence peddling incident where he and his followers poisoned participants in a political event. And on the extremely rare occasion that I lecture thugs on these subjects I often get a hearty laugh out of them by informing them that "The Playa from The Himalayas truly does exist."

From the point of having this Pimp Rajneesh pointed out to me by masters forward, in my incessant studies and ramblings the frequency of Indians in prominent pivotal positions and my discovery that things like numbers and all forms of mathematics were likewise of Indian invention, I took a targeted and very specific interest in what I eventually discovered was in fact an omni-dimensional culture with symbolism that is so broad that it encompasses everything from the symbolism of the US Government and its military and established political parties to the symbolism of the former Soviet Union to the symbolism of The Nazi menace, which borrowed more information, symbolism, technology and techniques from India than the average totally unthinking white supremacist knuckle-head can possibly even remotely begin to imagine, to our own pimpnological symbolism, which we like to think is very unique and specific to us, when in fact it is not, the Brahman Menace likewise has it and uses it everywhere.

If you study into the origins of modern civilization in depth, even mathematically or etymologically, it very quickly becomes crystal clear that virtually every aspect of modern civilization emerged from a single point, Sanskrit based Vedic culture...even Syntax, the core computer language that controls the entirety of modern civilization, is based on Sanskrit.

It is very interesting that if you travel the world as I have and engage people in conversation about the origins of their culture or nation more than half of them will tell you that, exactly as our culture, their culture likewise emerged from some element of omni-dimensional Indian culture...this is precisely why both Einstein and Oppenheimer famously quoted the Bhagavad Gita of The Mahabharata upon cracking the code to reengineering the technology to resurrect the nuclear weapon which I am completely convinced was reengineered and tested at the turn of the Century during the infamous Tunguska Event / Nuclear Explosion which was a Nuclear weapon pattern aerial detonation that was estimated to have been equivalent to 10 to 15 million tons of TNT that leveled 770 square miles of Siberian forest in late June of 1908.

It's why upon capturing Berlin and subsequently capturing all of the Nazi Stooge's stolen treasure troves the KGB used the 5,000 year old Dharma Marga yogic martial arts charts that they recovered to resurrect ancient Indian martial arts systems that are now called Aryan Martial Arts which the Russian Government teaches to its most capable secret agents today and its why if you get on any computer and type in True Aryans or Real Aryans, Indians will appear, because white people, who'd never heard of Aryanism prior to the emergence of Adolf Hitler and his Nationalist Socialist Worker's Party, are too young, inconsiderate, inexperienced and completely petrified out of their minds to be in control of the random campaigns that they are used carry out.

Contrary to popular belief, in sober reality, white people absolutely are not in control of the planet, they are in fact in third to fourth tier control of the planet at best and it is beyond any and all shadow of question and doubt my grand inquisitor level theologian lineage master pimpnological conclusion that white people have in reality merely been being used by The Brahman Menace, whom I am sure genetically engineered their race (which literally appeared right out of nowhere in The Middle East) as a white smokescreen to shield the Brahman Menace with the use of gene splicing or DNA code programming technology from a previous civilization during a period of revolutionary medical advancement when people foresaw and heavily debated the possibility of genetically engineering entire armies of troops that the Brahmans (Genies) collected and stored in hidden libraries, to advance yet another phase of their relentless bid for complete global conquest.

Given the fact that human beings don't have the coordination, attention span or mental capacity to conduct highly complex, extremely precise multi-millennial operations like these in the distance behind this Brahman Menace I can clearly see the silhouette of a non-humanoid female that is thousands of years old who has to reside in a completely isolated environment and have a team of caretakers enabling The Brahman Menace. This is perhaps the entity that we know of mythologically as Satan, who is purported to have deceived the whole world and who is believed to reside two hundred miles in the planetary core.

It is further my conclusion that it is extremely likely that even the Brahman Menace itself was genetically engineered, exactly as I also strongly suspect that the Asian race was genetically engineered at some point, perhaps during the Black Planet Phase of human history, during which someone concluded that it literally takes a continent of manpower and resources to conquer a continent of manpower and resources and rather than to try to work with inevitably problematic allies they would genetically engineer an entire continent of allies of their own and indoctrinate them from the ground up.

Every culture on Earth has a very different philosophical and tactical approach to conducting military operations and it is far beyond clear to me that the Brahman philosophical and tactical approaches are to employ their marked capabilities of total infiltration to play any situation from both ends and the middle. It is also clear to me that to finance the staggering cost of these ultra-complex inter-continental covert guerilla operations they would have a need to create phantom arms of the government like the Federal Reserve and Internal Revenue Service both of which are strongly suspected of being private banks (that could only be owned by Brahmans who are totally unequalled in the area of fronting and running dummy businesses to hide the true ownership of their investments and vastness of their wealth) and not government entities as is commonly believed and with the use of these extremely complex catalysts they could at least functionally get several continents of individuals to mindlessly do their bidding and mindlessly progress their sadistic aims.

As I've discussed these conclusions with various groups of people, I have found that it never fails to entertain, especially Chinese, who are well aware that white people are being used by someone else, that when presented with these facts, whites, who are the youngest race on Earth and ultimately have no real experience being considerate, absolutely cannot bring themselves to even remotely begin to imagine that through secret organizations they have long been being controlled by Indians, they are unknowingly obsessed with all things Indian from Indo-Arabic mathematics to Yoga to industry to global militarism and they unknowingly subconsciously in fact worship Indians whom employ whites more than anyone else on the planet.

I must add that it is absolutely astounding to me that the white race has been so perfectly framed for dreaming up and carrying out the innumerable overt and covert atrocities that they are invariably the front page news type face of, such as the North American Slave Trade, which was the largest and most murderous forced migration in the world's recorded history, the North American Indian and South American Inca and Aztec Indian Genocides and Massacres, the Namibian Holocaust that immediately preceded the European Holocausts carried out under Stalin and Hitler, the world war two Atomic Bombing of Japanese civilians when there was a standing army in the field and the post war refusal to medically treat Japanese civilians, and the Vietnam War era genocide and massacres to name a few, that absolutely no one believes that they are more guilty of than they themselves and it is stranger yet that many of these atrocious acts are found recorded in ancient jungle art and prophecies from religious works like the Holy Bible.

The ability to plan, covertly finance, coordinate and effectively execute plans that are as broad and covert as these and manage to keep those plans effectively hidden from the entire global populace is by no means or measure new kid on the block type shit, the intelligence to genetically engineer entire continents of people, create their entire cultures and effectively reduce them to ragdolls who mindlessly do the bidding of their invisible masters and run governments through back channels into the seats of a nation's halls of power by using secret organizations, which both the Catholic Church and several medieval European governments like Germany tried to prevent by outlawing secret organizations, take multiple human civilizations to organize and execute effectively, but I can see where it would be worth it because the yield is an entire continent of people who whole-heartedly embrace your culture because they have never had anything else whatsoever to embrace.

I also find it very interesting that it has been medically discovered that we have in excess of a billion brain cells which would both individually and collectively give us literally infinite lifespan and intellectual capacity and it is in fact only our density that stands between us and immortality, once this barrier is transcended we will be able to transcend the eight hundred year death barrier and ascend far beyond our present mythological era of sustained sub-enlightenment that we have repetitively not been allowed to exceed to an age of deification. However, my question has long been, who or what has limited both our life span and intellectual capacity to 10% when it is capable of functioning at 90% greater, in fact, at an infinite, capacity?

Another of my grand inquisitor level theologian lineage master pimpnological conclusions is that when you are aware of the fact that our suspiciously perfectly positioned moon, which there could not be life on this planet without, is an artificial satellite that is wholly composed of non-naturally occurring materials and you observe the mysterious and completely counter-reactionary functioning of humanity and all other entities of our planet, it becomes clear that we are functioning as integral components of a gigantic software program of some type and our little planet, which is suspiciously the only place in the solar system that can support our form of life, is in fact a completely artificial environment.

It is one of my most radical conclusions that man (as well as all other forms of life on the planet) is ultimately a form of artificial intelligence, a form of bio-electromagnetic, bio-degradable, self-replicating, wholly programmable software that is apparently living on a remote military outpost of some kind and being used for some form of military experimentation by something that is non-humanoid and everything that we can perceive around us is all part of a great experiment.

I believe that this is the precise reason that we are experiencing the medical anomaly of death, because we are being genetically programmed to live longer and shorter lifespans during various human civilizations as someone or something is apparently attempting to gauge the optimum life cycle for the perfect biological weapon.

I believe that we perish so easily and can make no mark within this ceaselessly self-generating environment because we absolutely are not a factor here, it is extremely possible that everything that we are able to perceive of as reality is just a temporal illusory component of a grand experiment that, just as any experiment, will eventually be scrapped.

It is also very interesting that, observing today's so-called war on terror, even though the United States Government has a mountain of intelligence and other evidence that terrorist insurgents are operating out of India and Pakistan, just as in the days of old, offensives always halt right at the door of India.

If average global citizens knew a bit of religious history, they could very quickly figure out that the traditional mortal enemy of Islam is in fact Hindus, not Christians, and this Afghanistan that the world's global super-powers can't seem to stop mortally embarrassing themselves fighting over is in fact India's long ago lost holy region of Hindustan that they had been playing both ends and the middle (by controlling both the terrorists and counter-terrorists western super-powers that are nothing more than Indian Satellite nations) to get back and they are now in fact being welcomed back into Hindustan with open arms by the Afghans.

This is precisely the core primary reason that there is never ending violence in the Middle East, because many flash points in The Middle East are right on the border of India, which is the most militant culture in the world, a culture that is so militant that it has the totally unparalleled ability to militarize anything from race to gender to human sexuality to religion to national boundaries and a militant culture that doesn't want anything around it, including China, that has any knowledge of its hideous history and tactics and can clearly identify it as the source of everything that we have ever been able to even remotely begin to imagine as civilization at any point in the history of the world. This is why it has been necessary to completely decimate every ancient indigenous culture in the world and it's why the libraries of Iran have been looted many times over again.

As a grand inquisitor level theologian lineage master predator who is quite aware that in the real world 1% is complete controlling interest,10% is religious controlling interest and 51% is financial controlling interest, it is very interesting to me, as a uniquely Brahman anomaly, that if one is observant, one will notice that, not only is there a disproportionately large number of Nobel Laureate recipients from India than there are from any other third world country, but these Nobel Laureate citations have all been awarded for discoveries of highly refined, cutting edge technologies which are all in reality merely re-engineered Indian technology from previous civilizations.

One will likewise notice that in any field in which Indians have a presence, they are never behind you, they are either right there with you, or they are far ahead of you, or they are far ahead of you, pretending to be right there with you... As a few prime examples, Indian scientists, who compose 20% of America's combined advanced research and technology sector in all fields, invented a large part of our present understanding of electromagnetics and they have discovered Algae as a revolutionary solution to the world's problems with carbon monoxide emissions.

In the telecom technical arena, Indians are coming up fast in the manufacture of cellphones and tablets, which are merely flat screen versions of the mythological Krystal Ball.

In the IT and Computer Programming Field, India is the computer language coding center of the world and they are coding everything from video games to surgical robots to state of the art modern aircraft in languages that we in The Western Hemisphere are not even familiar with. And when it comes to religion, whenever lectures are given on highly complex points of The Holy Koran or The Holy Bible, the most in depth and pinpoint precisely accurate lecturers on pivotal points of The Holy Koran and The Holy Bible are always Indian and they are never Muslims or Christians, they are invariable Brahmans or Sikhs...

Even Master Wallace Fard Muhammad, the founder of African American's Nation of Islam, was in fact an extremely shady Indo-Pakistani character with a plethora of aliases that both emerged from and disappeared into the shadows like so many other Invisible Imperial Masters whom have done everything from found religions and technologies to build pyramids, sun dials and all manner of techno-religious monuments in every corner of the world.

And when it comes to business, mathematics or medicine, globally, Indians, who invented numbers, most advanced mathematics, **Indo**-china, the **Indo**-European family of languages, the concepts of Mass-**indo**ctrination, scribes and news media moguls, **indus**trialization, the **military-indus**trial complex, recycling, highly advanced martial arts, chess and acupuncture, stand head and shoulders above all other practitioners in their given fields...

As a completely indefatigable student of history, it has long been very interesting to me that in an apparently illogical and completely senseless quagmire like Vietnam so many European nations (Brahman Satellites) were drawn into Southeast Asia on either side of the conflict to attempt to gain a foothold in Southeast Asia which has long been fought over for its fertility and strategic positioning and has recently been fought over because of the French built roads and ports that again made it a totally irresistible strategic foothold for a thrust into mainland China and ultimately for Brahman final conquest of the Asian Continent, not to mention to test new versions of ancient weapons like helicopters and other systems that were being employed to solve the age-old problems of over-extension of supply lines and the menace of reinforcement of fresh troops by an enemy by delivering then newly devised, illegal, inescapable, automated killing machines like C130 Puff The Magic Dragon that was capable of laying down 24,000 rounds per minute and was designed to kill so swiftly and efficiently that it would literally annihilate the enemy so fast that they would effectively be murdered beyond their troop replacement rate and inevitably be completely incapacitated of their ability to effectively wage war.

Since the Seventies America has been in a decline phase as America and indeed the whole of modern civilization is in the process of being systematically shut down. Though many of us do not like to think of humanity as being herded like domesticated animals, the fact is that we are in fact being herded like domesticated animals. Though many don't believe it, there is in fact a thing called "The Invisible Empire" that is very real and encompasses everything from the Islamic extremist paralleled hybrid religion of The Ku Klux Klan to the Justice System to the global banking system to The United Nations to all of the major religions.

Though this may sound outlandish and even flat out ridiculous to many of you, if one considers the abnormalities of human history it becomes clear very quickly that something is horribly out of place about several aspects of our present life on this planet. For example, if we have been wandering around this planet for anywhere from nine to sixty five million years, then why are technologies like flight and space travel only one hundred years old? And even more oddly, why are flight and many other technical capabilities written of in multiple thousand year old works all over the planet? And why is it that each and every one of those works, without a single exception, are solely religious works?

It is likewise extremely strange that all of the global superpowers who fought in the various "Theatres of War" during World Wars I and II were allies for Centuries before the wars and acted as enemies in the given "Theatres of War" during the wars have all, without a single exception, emerged as global **indus**trial superpowers after the wars were completed and all of these exact same superpowers mysteriously have chronologically directly parallel military histories and even today work very closely in every conceivable conflict that has occurred since the great wars.

What a completely stunning set of totally inconceivable coincidences!

It is even more stunningly coincidental yet that all of these superpowers, without a single exception, have acquired their entire cultural basis from **Indus** Valley Sanskrit based civilization which is the core primary source of all of the religious, symbolic, aristocratic, linguistic, legal, mathematical, and technical insights and capabilities in the modern world.

What a totally stunning set of coincidences!

As a grand inquisitor level theologian of many aspects of religion I spent nearly three decades trying to figure out why the word Hebrew was defined as "One from beyond" and after as many years of research and meditation it became irrefutably clear to me that these "Mythological Hebrews" are in fact a group of people from beyond the last total destruction of human civilization and they have in fact been using several entire human civilizations worth of insight to completely control the whole of humanity and very mysteriously just happen to be on sight at the beginning and ending of every miraculous and tragic event on Earth to both initiate and terminate the given action.

What I'm ultimately getting at here is that the whole of humanity is in totally incontrovertible fact a huge herd of Guinea Pigs that have been being completely unwittingly controlled by Brahman Priests via secret organizations that have stood behind virtually every government on Earth for the full span of recorded history.

As a graphic example of the point that I am trying to clarify, if one was to get on the internet and type in the name of King George VI in Masonic Garb and select images, a lovely photo of King George VI in Masonic Regalia will appear, along with images of George Washington and several other notable members of The Masonic Society. However, as an individual who is descended from innumerable generations of both over and underworld secret organizations myself, I can tell you that what is commonly missed, even by Masons, when people view an image like this, is the fact that Masons are builders and as builders, they are the builders of society, not the administrators of it. The administrators of society are Indians who have emerged from the jungles of India to on-site oversee the hyper-**indus**trialization and grand transition of modern society.

While many people concluded that Jews from all over Europe were massacred in Nazi Concentration Camps in Poland as revenge for the cold blooded murder and $300,000,000,000.00 armed robbery of The Russian Romanov division of the single global family that composed The Imperial Aristocracy, on which the sun never set, and the total collapse of the general aristocracy during the French and Russian Revolutions, I have long concluded that The Jews were knocked off because they were in the way of exponentially more powerful Indians whom have now far outpaced Jews in terms of wealth and in all spheres of global influence.

There is absolutely no question in my mind that at some point in our potential 65,000,000 years of human history, a single highly advanced and subsequently interplanetary, extraterrestrial culture that is very likely governed from a highly mobile satellite like Elysium and specializes in extremely deadly, highly complex and virtually imperceptible sabotage, psychological viruses, indirect action, pinpoint precise timing, precipitated self-neutralization, indeterminably subtle diversion and inconceivably effective remote control of 500,000,000 quantities of individuals has managed to gain the ability to wipe out nearly the whole of humanity at will via a pole shift, accomplish an effective reset of human history and roll out its own concept of reality and thereby for all intents and purposes gain complete control of the entire planet and it has been able to maintain that control by periodically creating multi-millennial intellect and capability setbacks for the rest of the known world via precipitated poleshifts.

I can absolutely assure you beyond all shadow of question and doubt that it is no mere coincidence that the inexorable Phoenix that everyone thinks is an Eagle that has been encrusted upon the imperial flag and standard of every Empire from the Egyptian and Roman Empires to the Czarist Russian Empire to all three German Reichs to the inherent Fourth American Reich is in fact one and the same; these Imperial satellites all have symbolic uniformity because they all have a uniform set of masters behind them.

Unfortunately, many things that we think are mere utilities and institutions are in fact weapons that have been used for countless millennia to control all of humanity. At its nucleus, the Indus Valley Civilization modeled concept of a state is ultimately nothing more than an extremely elaborate criminal organization and everything that it imagines to do is purely criminal and it specializes in debilitating and devaluating large masses of people and keeping them completely defenseless and isolated from possession of anything of real value. And as much as racists like to blame white people for all of their problems and even claim that the white man is the devil the real fact is that white people are simply not old and insightful enough to be in control of the disaster that has been being suffered by all of humanity; these problems far preceded the emergence and temporary empowerment of the white race.

Though white people, whom have spent much of their recent existence functioning as a white smoke screen to mask Brahman aggression, are the face of ultimately suicidal international aggression, for millennium white people were agrarian cultural isolationists who dwelled in the Caucuses and eventually Europe who farmed, bred, bothered absolutely no one and in fact never knew anything of class, caste, calculation, super weapons, Swastikas, Aryanism, Aristocracy, **Indus** Valley **Indus**trialization or attempted global conquest, until these concepts were presented to them by Indians.

As a matter of fact American Indians are called Indians because Columbus was trying to find a shorter route to India when he found America by mistake and even colonialism wasn't initiated until the Portuguese made it to India to receive insight / instructions and very interestingly even today, as the entire global economy steadily goes under, India is steadily rising and while other nations are toying with completely valueless and exponential debt accumulating digital and cellulose based wealth the broad mass of true value forms of wealth like gold are steadily flowing to and being accumulated and concentrated in India.

What I am ultimately getting at here is the totally incontrovertible fact that humanity as a species has been completely hacked and we many not be as high on the food chain as we like to believe that we are.

In our planetary history the world has in fact long been being ruled from The Asian Sub-continent, which along with The Horn of Africa, have been the general center of control of the entire planet for multiple human civilizations that has remained in control of the world even through multiple nearly entire human extinctions and what many people absolutely have not realized is that it is in fact huge influxes of Indians that has long driven seismic shifts in global intellectual, technological, militant and medical culture and this has proved true everywhere from Weimar Republic and Nazi Era Germany to the Middle East to the increasing global militancy of America and Great Britain to the emergence of Apartheid and Boko Haram in Africa to the heroin epidemics in both North and South America all of which were directly preceded by huge influxes of Indians who tend to eventually make up 10% of the academic, economical, industrial and medical elite in countries that they have very subtly highly influenced, seismically shifted and eventually completely unnoticeably managed to gain complete control of while not getting caught up in any dysfunctional social trends like divorce or drawing any attention to themselves.

The Omnipresent Elephant in the global room that no one has noticed throughout human history is in fact India and its Brahman and Sikh Intellectual, Industrial and Militant Agents who have brought about grand global cultural shifts like state sanctioned racism, Apartheid, Aryanism, radical-feminism, colonialism, religious and monetary based radicalism, terrorism, epidemic drug addiction and narco-terrorism that absolutely none of the nations like Germany, South Africa, Uganda, Nigeria and Kenya, that have embraced these ideals, had ever known anything of until they experienced a huge influx of Indians and ancient militant Indian ideas and objectives which invariably made the cultures of those countries completely unrecognizable as they have evolved into India exactly as has happened in North America which has become completely unrecognizable since we have experienced huge influxes of Indians and Pakistanis since the 60s and the only thing that has ever solved these problems is the expulsion of the Indians, Pakistanis and people who have been highly influenced by those highly militant cultures that have managed to infiltrate the cultural, intellectual, industrial, medical and military infrastructures of all of the very swiftly totally unrecognizable cultures into which they and their radical ideologies have been accepted.

Fully realizing that a gun will kill the man who made it, for innumerable millennia these priests have used extremely complex equations to set up layers of control of the whole of humanity in the form of institutions such as law, finance, marriage, militarism and religion upon which the entirety of human civilization have been built and when the priests are ready to liquidate a given entire civilization they merely rip this foundation out from beneath the given civilization thereby precipitating its inevitable collapse which is exactly what is occurring around the world today.

Our obsession with speed is inspiring our total disintegration, women's extremely warped concepts of strength, masculinity and total independence are creating a gulf between the genders (which Indian families are not getting caught up in) that is so wide that it is totally disintegrating our families and in fact swallowing our entire civilization, corporations mortal obsession with producing bigger figures has completely numbed them to the irrevocable fate of humanity and so we are deadlocked into a pre-formulated and mathematically equated conclusion and "The Black Girl Curse" has merely been a spearhead into the strategically precipitated total disintegration and inevitable collapse of yet another entire human civilization.

This is why Armageddon occurs in Revelations in The Holy Bible, because when it is revealed that a single culture is responsible for all of the misery that humanity has experienced in recorded history, combined international forces attempt to wipe out The Brahman Aristocracy which invariably escapes via a pre-prepped precipitated pole shift.

This is precisely the reason that every major **indus**trial nation on the face of the Earth is situated right next to a large body of water, so that when the shift inevitably occurs the whole of the **indus**trialized world will be completely wiped off of the face of the Earth and the Brahmans will have again covered their tracks and survived to implement another phase of operations just as they have done for God only knows how many millennia given that these operations are generally carried out in several thousand year increments.

This is why no one can tell what year it is, because given that the Brahmans and their operatives are in control of so many religions and governments they've been able to organize a completely dizzying array of timetables that keep everyone guessing at what date and time it really is.

It is a very grim reality of this world that ancient civilizations don't always remain in the past. It is a totally incontrovertible fact that if an extremely determined ancient totalitarian government was to be allowed to exist long enough it could in fact evolve into what Dr. Michio Kaku has described as a Type 4 Civilization that could in fact very realistically exist in the past, present and future simultaneously as a totally indestructible force in this world.

This kind of highly developed civilization could easily remotely control today's modern nations that are so young, inconsiderate, inexperienced and so far behind that they think that they are in first place. This is in fact why we are all called monkeys, because we are nothing more than embryonic ultra-subcultures by comparison.

This same Dr. Kaku has referred to the H1B Genius Visa that America uses to bring genius level students, engineers, scientists and researchers from other Countries to America to help us develop our highly advanced technology as America's Secret Weapon. However, I must diametrically disagree with Dr. Kaku on that single point...

America, along with the entirety of the industrialized world, is in fact merely one among many satellites of India's exceedingly ancient Brahman Aristocracy which functions as the invisible and subsequently invincible empire from which our entire modern hyper-industrialized reality is streaming and given this, American in fact does not have a secret weapon in the form of the H1B Visa, this secret weapon is in fact India's, who has remained in remote control of the entirety of human civilization for innumerable millennium.

These H1B Visa people have to come over here and help us with the development of things like the development of super-advanced electronics, medical techniques and the further development of our space program because neither these highly advanced technologies or the space program are our technology or space program, they are in fact India's.

America got its space program from the Nazis and the Nazis got their advanced technology and space program straight from the libraries of India's Brahman Aristocracy whom were the super-wealthy so-called Jews that revolutionized Germany's entire culture during Weimar Republic Era Germany.

Japan also imported members of The Brahman Aristocracy to their country to help Japan build its modern industries and economy... Our minuscule 100 year techno-industrial miracle of a modern civilization is ultimately nothing more than a highly elaborate prop that is part of an extremely ancient recycling program that is centered around maintaining Complete Control of the planet and its entire populace for innumerable generations.

Given that these people specialize in precipitating, remotely controlling, subtly invading and eventually completely strangling adolescent cultures to death, what has not been realized by re-incarnated, incubated and remotely controlled embryonic ultra-sub-cultures like America, which are so far behind that they think that they are in first place, is the fact that, at this very moment, as a global civilization, we are in fact in a mortal struggle for our lives with the invisible and apparently invincible arms of ancient, totally inconceivably multifaceted, India, which, in the interest of maintaining Complete Control and Global Conquest, is in the process of regressing us back to the stone age which, in the absence of modern amenities, is only two weeks away and our gross lack of awareness of these facts as a global civilization are in fact totally unsurvivable ignorance!

A SINGLE SOLUTION

<u>KEEP POSING UNTIL YOU'RE FROZEN, AND THEN DO WHAT MUST BE DONE!</u>

THE WHOLE AND SOLE point of this book has ultimately been that there in fact is enough space and opportunity for all of us and we can in fact all live together and we can in fact do so in peace, the only problem that has caused this not to happen in memorable history is that instead of being satisfied with their piece of the pie, the Brahman Menace has been mortally obsessed with having the whole pie solely for themselves and over the millennia they have managed to devised some extremely creative means of accomplishing this and they will stop at absolutely nothing until they have accomplished their sadistic goal of absolute and complete global domination and until all of humanity uses our combined global intelligence and resources to once and for all put a stop to this menace, which is in fact the true global terrorist, humanity will never have anything that even remotely resembles peace or sensibility.

The information in this book, which resurfaces about every 5,000 years, is in fact the master key to understanding why the secret organizations that run major governments through back channels exist, what information they are trying to protect and how this is directly linked to hatred of blacks that is a direct product of the fact that time and time again black priests have been able to uncover the Brahman Menace and ultimately lead the charge to put a stop to it.